THE SMALL BUSINESS PLAYBOOK

THE ULTIMATE BEGINNER'S GUIDE: PRACTICAL STEPS TO BECOME A PROFITABLE BUSINESS OWNER

PETE SRODOSKI

TABLE OF CONTENTS

INTRODUCTION

"It had long since come to my attention that people of accomplishment rarely sat back and let things happen to them. They went out and happened to things."
— Leonardo da Vinci

Welcome, my friend, to the unseen world of small business ownership. A place where entrepreneurial dreams meet the gritty realities of daily operations. The journey of an entrepreneur is often romanticized, but as someone who has walked that path, I can tell you that it's a lot more challenging and less glamorous than it appears at first.

Running a small business isn't just about turning a profit; it's more about leading a team, navigating complex problems, and constantly adapting to an ever-changing marketplace. Yet, despite these challenges, it's one of the most rewarding endeavors one would ever undertake.

Did you know that small businesses make up 99.9% of all businesses in the United States? They're the lifeblood of our economy, as they are creating two-thirds of all new jobs. That's the power of small businesses, and that's the power you hold as a business owner.

This isn't just a playbook; it's a guide, a friend, and a mentor, which will help you navigate the complexities of running a small business. I've been where you are, faced the struggles you're facing, and came out successfully. I've learned a lot along the way, and I want to share these insights with you.

I've served as the CEO and COO of multiple businesses, managing revenues of up to $100 million and more annually, but I've also been the guy working late into the night, trying to figure out the budget for the next quarter. I've celebrated big wins, and I've also faced crushing defeats. I've hired some really brilliant people, and I have also been burned by some of those closest to me. Through it all, I've learned valuable lessons that I believe can help you on your journey.

So, whether you're a seasoned business owner or just starting out, I invite you to join me on this journey. Let's explore the owner's path together, from startup to success, and uncover the practical strategies, insights, and tools you'll need to take your business to the next level.

CHAPTER 1:
FROM VISION TO REALITY

"Good business leaders create a vision, articulate the vision, passionately own the vision, and relentlessly drive it to completion."
– Jack Welch

1.1 CRAFTING A COMPELLING VISION

The first step to successful small business leadership is crafting a compelling vision. It's the North Star that guides you, the beacon that keeps you on track when the seas of business get stormy. It's not a mission statement you tack on your website or an elevator pitch you rehearse for your in-laws. Your vision is the bedrock upon which your business is built, the guiding principle that informs every decision you make.

I like to think of your vision as a roadmap to success. You get to decide the direction your company is headed. For some people, that can be incredibly daunting and for others, it can be the coolest part of being a business owner. Close your eyes for a moment (unless you're driving or running on the treadmill) and envision the last time you were on a flight. Do you see the plots of land, the mountains, and the forests? That should be your viewpoint of your business while crafting the vision. You should be able to see everything in totality.

With the ability to see your business as a whole, it will be exponentially easier to craft your company's vision. Think of it like this: where do I want to go? That means understanding the end goal of this thing you've created. Do you want to grow into a worldwide powerhouse? A regional juggernaut? Or are you simply satisfied with running a business that will allow you to do what you love and get paid for it? The ultimate question when visioning is, "why am I doing what I am doing?" Answer that and you'll have your vision.

Identifying Core Values

Embarking on the journey of identifying your core values is a fundamental step in defining the character and ethos of your business. These are the non-negotiable principles that form the foundation of your business operations, the values you unwaveringly adhere to. Whether it be unwavering integrity, relentless innovation, or exceptional customer service, these core values differ from one business to another. Yet, they are uniformly recognized and deeply ingrained in the hearts of successful business owners.

To effectively determine your core values, consider the qualities you would seek in an ideal employee. Think about the characteristics that are essential for someone representing your company. Would you value their ability to follow directions meticulously, their genuine care for team dynamics, their prioritization of others, or their capacity to lead with empathy? These reflections are a mirror to your core values.

However, identifying your core values transcends merely listing admirable traits. It involves an introspective and sometimes challenging process of understanding not just what you stand for, but also what you unequivocally reject. It's about drawing a definitive line in the sand, and declaring unequivocally, "This is who we are, and just as importantly, this is who we are not." This clarity guides every decision, every hire, and every strategic direction your business takes.

Establishing your core values is akin to setting a moral compass for your business. It is about making tough decisions and maintaining those standards, especially when faced with situations that tempt compromise. In essence, your core values are more than just words; they are a commitment to a set of principles that define every aspect of how your business operates and interacts with the world. They are the guiding lights that illuminate your path in the business world, ensuring that every step taken aligns with the essence of what your business truly represents.

Defining Business Purpose

After establishing your core values, the next pivotal step is to define your business purpose. This goes beyond the mere mechanics of what your business does; it delves into the why. Why does your business exist? What unique problem are you solving? How are you enriching the lives of your customers? Your business purpose is not about the products or services you offer; it's about the reasons and motivations behind them.

Understanding your business purpose can range from straightforward goals like "supporting the local community" to more specific objectives like "providing advanced x-ray machines to hospitals in northwest Minnesota." The essence of identifying your purpose is to maintain a clear focus. It helps to steer your team away from the distractions of fleeting opportunities or those 'shiny objects' that do not align with your core mission.

Consider a local coffee shop owner as an example. Her business purpose transcends the mere selling of coffee. Instead, it's about creating a space that fosters community connections and conversations. In this case, the coffee shop becomes a conduit for achieving a higher goal - a hub for communal interaction and warmth. The coffee, while integral, is a means to an end, not the end itself.

In other words, defining your business purpose is about uncovering the deeper impact and value your business brings to its customers and community. It's the underlying force that drives every decision, shapes your brand, and differentiates you in the market. This clarity in purpose not only guides your business strategy but also resonates with your customers, employees, and stakeholders, hence, creating a more meaningful and connected business experience.

Visualizing Future Success

Next is to visualize your future success. This isn't about daydreaming about your business on the cover of Forbes or fantasizing about that beach house you'll buy when you retire. It's about clearly picturing what success looks like for your business.

Think about where you want your business to be in one year, five years, ten years, etc. What products or services are you offering? What kind of customers are you serving? How many employees do you have? What kind of culture does your company have?

Make this visualization as detailed as possible. Write it down, draw it, create a vision board. The more vivid your visualization is, the more powerful it will be in guiding your business decisions.

Aligning Vision with Market Reality

Finally, align your vision with market reality. This isn't about diluting your vision to fit the market; it's about finding the intersection of your vision and the market need.

You may have a vision of creating the world's first zero-gravity coffee shop, but if the market for zero-gravity coffee is non-existent, you'll need to adjust your vision. Conversely, if you see a gap in the market for eco-friendly coffee shops, you might adjust your vision to fill that gap.

Remember, your vision is a guiding principle, not a fixed destination. It should be flexible enough to adapt to changing market conditions, but strong enough to keep you grounded in your core values and business purpose.

So often people get bogged down trying to turn their dreams into a business. Sadly, if your dreams have little-to-no demand, then you need to continue looking. I would recommend getting your business profitable first and then using your additional resources on your passion.

Take the time to craft a compelling vision, as it's an investment in your business's future success, and one of the most important steps you can take as a business owner. Your vision will guide you, inspire you, and keep you focused on the road ahead. It's the first step in turning your entrepreneurial dreams into reality, and it all starts with you.

1.2 TRANSLATING VISION INTO STRATEGY

Setting Strategic Objectives

With your vision now clearly defined and firmly anchored in your mind, the next crucial step is to transform this vision into a tangible and actionable strategy. This transformation begins with the setting of strategic objectives. These objectives are specific, measurable, and time-bound goals that are in direct alignment with your vision, serving as the catalysts that drive your business forward.

Consider your vision as the destination in a journey, and your strategic objectives as the crucial steps or milestones along the path to that destination. They are the concrete actions and targets that provide direction and momentum as you work towards realizing your vision. For instance, if your vision is to become the leading eco-friendly coffee shop in your community, a strategic objective could be to source 100% of your coffee beans from sustainable farms within a specific timeframe, say the next two years.

These objectives are more than just lofty aspirations; they are actionable commitments that lay out a clear roadmap for your business. They help break down the grand vision into achievable chunks, hence, making the journey towards your ultimate goal less daunting and more structured. By setting these strategic objectives, you not only provide your team with clear direction but also establish benchmarks to measure progress and success.

In essence, setting strategic objectives is about creating a bridge between your current position and the future you envision for your business. It involves thoughtful planning, realistic goal-setting, and a commitment to tracking and adjusting these goals as necessary. This process ensures that every step taken brings you closer to realizing your vision, keeping your business on a steady and purposeful course towards success.

Analyzing Market Trends

As you're setting your strategic objectives, it's crucial to analyze market trends. What's happening in your industry? What are your competitors doing? What are your customers demanding? What are the emerging trends that could affect your business?

For our coffee shop owner, she might notice a growing demand for plant-based milk alternatives or a rising trend of remote workers seeking co-working spaces. These trends could inform her strategic objectives and shape her business strategy.

Keep in mind that market trends are dynamic; they change and evolve. Therefore, it's essential to stay informed and regularly update your market analysis.

Your best option is to follow groups on social media, get involved with masterminds, and just ask questions from people in the industry. I've found that people are typically very generous with information if you could just ask. This will give you the confidence that you're heading in the right direction.

Identifying Competitive Advantage

Next, identify your competitive advantage. What sets you apart from your competitors? Why should customers choose you over others? The answer to these questions form your competitive advantage. I frequently refer to your competitive advantage as the differentiators that you need to focus on to set you apart from the crowd.

You might offer a unique product, exceptional customer service, or a memorable in-store experience. Your competitive advantage could also be your commitment to sustainability and ethically sourced products. Whatever it is, your competitive advantage should be something that your competitors can't easily replicate.

Our eco-friendly coffee shop owner, for example, might find her competitive advantage in her strict adherence to sustainable practices, setting her apart from other coffee shops that only partially commit to sustainability.

Designing a Unique Value Proposition

The final step in translating your vision into a tangible reality is designing your unique value proposition (UVP). This critical element is a succinct statement that articulates how your product or service addresses the specific needs of your customers, offers distinct benefits, and importantly, delineates why customers should choose you over your competitors.

At its core, your UVP is the pledge you make to your customers. It encapsulates what sets you apart in the marketplace and provides a compelling reason for customers to select your brand. It's the essence of what makes your business unique and desirable.

To develop a truly effective UVP, a deep and intimate understanding of your customer base is essential. You need to have a comprehensive grasp of their desires, challenges, and aspirations. This knowledge allows you to craft a UVP that not only resonate with them but also speaks directly to their needs and expectations.

Consider, for example, our eco-friendly coffee shop. Its UVP could be: "Savor the unique experience of enjoying a cup of coffee that's as good for the planet as it is for you. At our café, we proudly serve 100% sustainably sourced coffee in an ambiance that's both inviting and environmentally conscious. With every sip, you're making a positive impact."

By shaping your vision into a strategy through the creation of a UVP, you begin the journey of turning your entrepreneurial dreams into reality. It's crucial to remember that while a vision without a strategy might remain a mere dream, a vision underpinned by a solid strategy has the power to make a significant impact. Your UVP is not just a statement; it's a strategic tool that bridges the gap between where you are and where you want to be, hence, changing the world one step at a time.

1.3 BUILDING A ROBUST BUSINESS PLAN

Market Analysis

Let's move on to the market analysis. This is where you'll examine your industry, your competition, and your target customers. You'll start by defining your industry. What is its size? What's its growth rate? What are the key trends and factors driving the industry?

Then, you'll analyze your competition. Who are they? What do they offer? How do they price their products or services? What are their strengths and weaknesses?

Finally, you'll dive into understanding your target customers. Who are they? What are their needs and wants? What influences their buying decisions?

This isn't just a data collection exercise. It's an opportunity to glean insights that will shape your business. For instance, if you discover that your competition is weak in customer service, it could be an opportunity for you to make a difference.

Business Model Design

Next, we'll design your business model. This outlines how your business creates, delivers, and captures value. Here, we'll define your key partners, activities, resources, value proposition, customer relationships, channels, customer segments, cost structure, and revenue streams.

Your business model isn't static; it should evolve as your business and the market changes. For instance, if you discover a new customer segment, you might modify your business model to cater to this segment.

Financial Projections

Embarking on financial projections is a crucial step in your business planning process. This is where you'll forecast your future sales, costs, and, ultimately, profits – providing a glimpse into the financial viability of your business.

Begin with your sales projections. Consider the number of products or services you anticipate selling each month and how you expect these figures to evolve over time. This initial step sets the stage for understanding your potential revenue streams.

Next, shift your focus to estimating expenses, both fixed and variable. Fixed expenses are the unavoidable costs that recur monthly, essential for keeping your business operational, such as rent, utilities, and salaries. On the other hand, variable expenses fluctuate with your business activities. These include marketing costs, travel expenses, conference attendance fees, and similar outlays. The key here is to capture all the costs associated with producing and delivering your product or service.

Once you have a clear picture of your total expenses, you can then drill down to one of the most critical aspects of your projections: profit. This is determined by subtracting your total costs from your sales figures. If the resulting profit margin is lower than desired or dips into the negative, it's a signal to reassess – perhaps by scaling back variable expenses or by setting a higher sales target.

It's important to remember that these financial projections are, by nature, estimates. They won't be exact and will likely need adjustments as real-world data and experience come into play. However, they are invaluable in providing a preliminary assessment of the financial health of your business. These projections are not just numbers on a spreadsheet; they're a strategic tool that guides decision-making and helps you gauge the feasibility and future direction of your business endeavor.

Risk Assessment

Risk is inherent in every business venture, so it's important to identify and plan for potential risks. This could include market risks, such as changes in consumer preferences, financial risks, such as fluctuations in currency exchange rates, operational risks, such as equipment failure, and more.

Once you've identified potential risks, develop strategies to mitigate them. For instance, you might diversify your product range to spread market risk, or establish a reserve fund to manage financial risk.

Marketing and Sales Strategy

Now, let's focus on crafting your marketing and sales strategy, which is a crucial component that dictates how you will attract and retain customers. This strategy is essentially your roadmap for making meaningful connections with your target audience and converting these connections into lasting customer relationships.

Your marketing strategy should be a dynamic blend of both online and offline methods. This might include a combination of social media engagement, email marketing campaigns, content marketing initiatives, search engine optimization tactics, traditional advertising, public relations efforts, and other relevant approaches. The key is to select methods that resonate most with your target customers' preferences and habits, ensuring your message reaches them effectively.

In contrast, your sales strategy should detail the mechanisms by which you'll transform potential leads into actual paying customers. Elements of this strategy could encompass your sales process, choice of sales channels, the structure and training of your sales team, and sales incentives that motivate and reward successful conversions.

At the heart of both your marketing and sales strategies should be a deep and nuanced understanding of your target customers. This isn't about casting a wide net to catch anyone and everyone; it's about strategically targeting and appealing to the right audience. Your strategy should be fine-tuned to address the specific needs, pain points, and aspirations of your ideal customers, ensuring that every marketing and sales effort is not just seen and heard but also felt and responded to.

Essentially, your marketing and sales strategy is more than a set of tactics; it's a coordinated, customer-centric approach that aligns your business objectives with the desires and needs of your market. By being thoughtful and targeted in these strategies, you set the stage for not just attracting customers but building lasting, valuable relationships with them.

1.4 TURNING STRATEGY INTO ACTION

With a solid strategy in place, it's time to roll up your sleeves and bring your plan to life. This is where the rubber meets the road, where your dreams take flight, and where the magic happens. But remember, it's not just enough to have a plan; you need to act on it. So, let's turn your strategy into action.

Setting SMART Goals

First things first, let's set some goals. But not just any goals - SMART goals. These are Specific, Measurable, Achievable, Relevant, and Time-bound.

Let's imagine you're running a boutique bakery. A vague goal might be, "I want to sell more cakes." But a SMART goal would be, "I want to increase cake sales by 20% over the next six months by introducing two new flavors and running a targeted social media campaign."

This goal is Specific (increase cake sales by 20%), Measurable (you can track cake sales), Achievable (with new flavors and marketing, this is realistic), Relevant (it aligns with your business objectives), and Time-bound (you've set a deadline of six months).

Developing an Action Plan

Next, let's develop an action plan. This is your roadmap for achieving your goals. It outlines the specific steps you need to take, who is responsible for each step, and when each step should be completed.

Using the bakery example, your action plan might include steps like researching popular cake flavors, testing new recipes, training staff on making the new cakes, developing a social media strategy, scheduling regular social media posts, and tracking sales of the new cakes.

Allocating Resources

Now, it's time to allocate resources. This involves determining what resources you'll need to execute your action plan and how you'll allocate them.

Resources could include money, time, staff, equipment, or supplies. For example, in the bakery, you might need to allocate a budget for ingredients and marketing, time for recipe testing and social media management, staff for baking and selling cakes, and kitchen space and equipment for making the cakes.

Remember, resources are finite. There is always an opportunity cost to allocating your resources. Using your time, resources, employees, and equipment on one priority prevents you from using it on a different one. It's important to use them wisely and ensure they're invested in activities that drive you closer to your goals.

Monitoring Progress

Finally, and perhaps most importantly, you'll need to monitor your progress. This involves regularly checking in on your goals, assessing your progress, and adjusting your plan as needed.

In the bakery scenario, you might track daily cake sales, monitor social media engagement rates, and collect customer feedback on the new cake flavors. If you find you're not making progress as expected, you might tweak the recipes, adjust the social media strategy, or offer a promotion to boost sales.

Monitoring progress isn't just about keeping track of numbers. It's about learning, adapting, and improving. It's about celebrating your wins, learning from your losses, and always striving to do better. Remember, numbers are just numbers unless you use them for something. Make sure that you are utilizing the numbers as a resource for leading and inspiring your team.

And with that, we've covered the process of turning strategy into action. Remember, a strategy without action is just a wish. But a strategy with action can change the world. So, take that strategy, turn it into action, and watch as your business transforms and grows.

Running a business is not a sprint; it's more of a marathon. You'll face hurdles, twists, and turns along the way. But with your vision in sight, a robust strategy on hand, and a willingness to take action, you're well on your way to creating a business that's not only profitable but also fulfilling and impactful. So, strap in, brace yourself, and get ready for an exciting ride. This is just the beginning, and the best is yet to come.

FROM VISION TO REALITY

- ☐ CRAFT A VISION

- ☐ DEFINE CORE VALUES & PURPOSE

- ☐ SET STRATEGIC OBJECTIVES

- ☐ DESIGN YOUR U.V.P.

- ☐ PROJECT YOUR FINANCIALS

- ☐ DEVELOP A SALES STRATEGY

- ☐ SET SMART GOALS & ACTION PLAN

CHAPTER 2:
FINANCIAL SAVVY FOR
THE NON-FINANCIAL BUSINESS OWNER

"We should remember that good fortune often happens when opportunity meets with preparation."
– Thomas A. Edison

Imagine yourself standing in front of a painting, a complex masterpiece of colors, shapes, and textures. At first glance, it might seem overwhelming, or even chaotic. But as you step closer, as you start to understand the artist's technique and perspective, the chaos then gives way to clarity. Suddenly, the painting comes to life, every brushstroke telling a story, every color evoking an emotion.

That's what understanding financial statements is like. At first, they might seem daunting - a jumble of numbers and jargon. But once you understand the language, once you learn to interpret the numbers, those financial statements become a powerful tool in your entrepreneurial toolkit. They offer you a glimpse into your business's financial health, helping you make informed decisions and chart a course for success.

When I first started looking at financial statements, they made absolutely no sense. Now, after decades in business, I can quickly glance at a company's P&L and tell you the areas the business is doing well and where their opportunities are.

2.1 UNDERSTANDING FINANCIAL STATEMENTS

Like a well-told story, financial statements capture and present your business's financial performance and condition in a structured and meaningful way. They are the language of business, and mastering them is crucial for a business owner. In this section, we will look at the four key elements of financial statements: the income statement, balance sheet, cash flow statement, and key financial ratios.

Income Statement Basics

Think of the income statement as the 'scorecard' of your business for a specific period. Also known as a profit and loss statement, it showcases your revenue (what you've earned), costs (what you've spent), and the resulting profit or loss (revenue minus costs).

Let's say you run a local bakery and your revenue comprises the sales from your delicious pastries and cakes. Your costs include the ingredients, wages for your staff, rent for your shop, utilities, and other expenses related to your operations. Subtract these costs from your revenue, and voila, you have your profit or loss.

Balance Sheet Analysis

Now, let's move on to the balance sheet. It provides a 'snapshot' of what your company owns (assets), owes (liabilities), and the net ownership (equity) at a specific point in time.

Going back to our bakery example, your assets could include your baking equipment, cash in the bank, and any unsold pastries. Your liabilities might be a business loan you've taken to buy that shiny new oven or money owed to suppliers for flour and butter. The difference between your assets and liabilities represents your equity, which is the net worth of your business.

Cash Flow Statement Insights

Next, we have the cash flow statement, which is a record of the cash entering and leaving your business over a period. It's divided into three sections: cash flows from operating activities (day-to-day business operations, like selling pastries), investing activities (buying or selling assets, like an oven), and financing activities (borrowing from or repaying investors or lenders).

In our bakery, if you sell more pastries, your cash inflow from operating activities increases. If you decide to buy a new oven, your cash outflow from investing activities increases. Taken together, these elements paint a picture of your business's liquidity - its ability to pay its bills.

Key Financial Ratios

Finally, we come to financial ratios, which are like vital signs for your business. They offer valuable insights into profitability, efficiency, liquidity, and solvency.

Let's explore a few key ratios. The gross profit margin, calculated from your income statement, shows how efficiently you turn raw materials (like flour and butter) into finished products (like pastries). The current ratio, derived from your balance sheet, gives you a sense of whether you have enough resources to cover your short-term obligations. The return on assets ratio, using information from both your income statement and balance sheet, measures how effectively you're using your assets to generate profits.

Remember, these ratios aren't just numbers but diagnostic tools. They can help you identify strengths to leverage and weaknesses to address.

In the world of business, financial statements are like a lighthouse guiding you through the foggy seas of entrepreneurship. Just as I mentioned earlier, they're not just numbers on a page; they're a narrative, a story that reveals where your business has been, where it stands now, and where it's headed. Understanding this story, and learning to interpret its nuances and subtleties is key to your success as a business owner. So, arm yourself with this knowledge, and let it light your path as you navigate the fascinating world of entrepreneurship.

The healthiest businesses I work with are the businesses that have a deep understanding of their financial situation. Knowing how your company is doing will give you the confidence to make key business decisions like, "when do we hire, how much can I provide for bonuses this year, and can I invest in this new tool?"

2.2 BUDGETING FOR BUSINESS SUCCESS

As a small business owner, you're a juggler, deftly balancing a myriad of responsibilities. Of all the balls you're keeping in the air, the budget is one of the most delicate. A slight misstep can send it crashing down. But with careful planning and management, budgeting can become a powerful ally in your quest for business success.

Revenue Forecasting

The first step in budgeting is to anticipate your revenue or the income your business will generate in a specific period. This is your starting line on the budget racetrack, which will mark the resources you have at your disposal.

In order to be able to forecast revenue, you need to look at your sales history, market trends, and business growth plans. Think of it as a weather forecast for your business. You're using past patterns, current conditions, and future predictions to anticipate what lies ahead.

Let's say you own a landscaping business. You'd look at your past contracts, consider seasonal trends (more work in spring and fall, less in summer and winter), and factor in any plans for expansion like new service offerings or territories.

Expense Planning

Once you've got your revenue forecast, you can move on to planning your expenses. This is the cost your business will incur to generate that forecasted revenue. It's the fuel your business needs to race towards its goals.

Your expenses could include salaries, rent, utilities, supplies, marketing costs, and more. It's important to categorize these into fixed costs (those that remain constant, like rent) and variable costs (those that fluctuate with business activity, like raw materials).

For our landscaping business, fixed costs could include office rent and insurance, while variable costs could include plants, mulch, and labor.

Cash Flow Management

Now, let's talk about cash flow management. This is the process of tracking when, where, and how your cash is coming in and going out of your business. It's like the heartbeat of your business, pumping the lifeblood (cash) through its veins (your business operations).

Effective cash flow management ensures that you always have enough cash to cover your expenses and invest in growth opportunities. It's about timing your income and expenses so that you're never left short of cash.

For instance, in our landscaping example, you might schedule your client payments to come in before you need to pay your suppliers. You might also arrange for staggered payment of large expenses to avoid a big cash outflow all at once.

During the years of COVID, I was running a frozen dessert business. We had assumed control of the business after the previous owner ran it into the ground. As a result, we faced heavy debt. Each week, my CFO and I went through our expenses and cash flow line-by-line to prioritize our primary expenditures.

Without a thorough cash flow forecast, we could never have known how much product to purchase, how to make payroll, or how to pay rent. An excellent cash flow forecast in times of crisis is key to keeping a business open instead of closing it.

Budget Review and Adjustment

Finally, budgeting isn't a set-it-and-forget-it process. It's a living, breathing tool that needs regular review and adjustment. Think of it as a fitness routine for your business. You wouldn't expect to get in shape with a single workout, would you? The same applies to your budget.

Regular reviews help you identify any deviations from your budget, allowing you to take corrective action before minor issues become major problems. Maybe your landscaping business has had a surge in demand, and you need more supplies than planned. Or perhaps a new competitor has entered the market, and you need to ramp up your marketing efforts.

Some owners I work with adjust their budget monthly, due to the volatile nature of their business. Others, however, don't change their plans all year. They have been operating for so long and their revenue and expenses are consistently achieved. It takes time to achieve this type of data for your business though. Don't stress if you haven't got it all figured out in the first year.

Adjustments, on the other hand, help you adapt your budget to changing business conditions. Maybe you've discovered a more cost-effective supplier, or perhaps you've decided to invest in new equipment to increase efficiency.

Budgeting may seem like a complex and daunting task, but it's truly a game-changer for your business. It equips you with the knowledge and control you need to make informed decisions, manage risks, and steer your business towards success. So, embrace the budgeting process, and let it guide you on your path to entrepreneurial victory.

2.3 MANAGING CASH FLOW

Accounts Receivable Management

Imagine a bustling marketplace, filled with vendors selling their wares. The air is thick with the promise of transactions-the exchange of goods for payment. In our digital age, this marketplace has expanded beyond physical boundaries, but the essence remains the same: you provide a product or service, and in return, you receive payment. This is the crux of accounts receivable management.

Accounts receivable represent the money owed to you by customers who have purchased your goods or services on credit. In an ideal world, as soon as you issue an invoice, the customer would promptly pay it. However, in reality, delays often occur. These delays can tie up your cash and strain your cash flow.

Effective accounts receivable management involves strategies to expedite these payments. This could include offering early payment discounts or imposing late payment penalties. You could also adopt a policy of conducting credit checks on new customers or require upfront deposits for large orders.

Think of it as a balancing act. On one side, you want to offer flexible payment options to attract and retain customers.

But on the other side, you need to ensure timely payments to maintain a healthy cash flow. Your challenge is to find that sweet spot where customer satisfaction meets cash flow stability.

Inventory Control

Now, let's turn our attention to inventory control. If you're in a product-based business, your inventory represents a significant portion of your assets. But inventory isn't just static boxes sitting in a warehouse, rather it is a dynamic part of your operations that directly impacts your cash flow.

Here's why: every item in your inventory ties up your cash until it's sold. The longer items sit on your shelves, the longer your cash is tied up. On the flip side, if you run out of a popular product, you could lose sales and customers.

Effective inventory control involves maintaining the right amount of inventory to meet customer demand without overstocking. This requires a keen understanding of your sales pattern and customer buying behavior. You'll also need systems for tracking inventory levels in real-time and triggering restocks at the right time.

Consider the case of a hardware store owner. If he notices that sales of gardening tools spike every spring, he might decide to increase his inventory of these items in the preceding months. On the other hand, if he finds that certain items are gathering dust on the shelves, he might choose to discontinue them to free up cash. Always remember, if it's in the back, then it's on a stack, and if it's on the floor, it goes out the door.

Accounts Payable Strategy

Next up is your accounts payable strategy. Accounts payable represents the money you owe to your suppliers for goods or services purchased on credit. While it might be tempting to delay these payments to conserve your cash, a more strategic approach can yield better results.

Crafting an effective accounts payable strategy involves negotiating favorable payment terms with your suppliers. This could mean longer payment periods or discounts for early payments. It's also crucial to prioritize your payments based on the importance of the supplier and the consequences of late payment.

Let's say you're running a restaurant. Your food suppliers are critical to your operations, and late payments could disrupt your supplies, hence, leading to dissatisfied customers. On the other hand, a delay in paying your cleaning service might not have immediate operational impacts. Therefore, you might prioritize payment to your food suppliers to ensure a smooth flow of ingredients for your culinary creations.

Typically, new relationships with vendors have shorter payment terms, which will give you and your business less time to pay that expense back. As your relationships with your vendors improve over time, ask for better payment terms to strengthen your buying potential.

Cash Flow Forecasting

Finally, we circle back to cash flow, but this time, we're looking ahead. Cash flow forecasting is the process of predicting your future cash inflows and outflows. It's like peering into a crystal ball, giving you a glimpse into your future financial position.

To accurately forecast your cash flow, you'll need to estimate your future sales, costs, and capital expenditures. It's important to factor in seasonal variations, planned investments, and potential risks.

For example, if you're a wedding planner, you might expect higher cash inflows during the wedding season and lower inflows during off-peak periods. If you're planning to invest in new office equipment, this would be a forecasted cash outflow.

Remember, your cash flow forecast is not set in stone. It's a dynamic tool that should be updated regularly to reflect changes in your business and the market. It serves as a guide, which helps you anticipate cash shortfalls or surpluses and plan accordingly.

Managing cash flow is a critical part of running a small business, as it's about striking a balance between incoming and outgoing cash, keeping enough cash on hand to cover your costs, and investing in growth. With effective accounts receivable management, inventory control, accounts payable strategy, and cash flow forecasting, you can navigate the financial ebbs and flows of your business with confidence.

2.4 PROFITABILITY: MORE THAN JUST REVENUE

Running a thriving business is akin to cooking a perfect meal. You need the right ingredients, the right recipe, and the right timing. In the case of your business, the primary ingredient for profitability is not just revenue but understanding and managing your margins and returns effectively.

Gross Profit Margin Analysis

Let's start with the gross profit margin. This is the percentage of total sales revenue that your company retains after incurring the direct costs associated with producing the goods and services sold by your company. It's the percentage of each dollar of a company's revenue available after accounting for the cost of goods sold (COGS).

Consider the case of a widget retailer. Each widget sold incurs costs such as the purchase price from the manufacturer, shipping, and custom fees. By subtracting these costs from the sales price, you ascertain the gross profit. The gross profit margin is this profit expressed as a percentage of the sales price. A higher percentage indicates that your company retains more of each dollar of sales, which means more money for other operational expenses and net profit.

Net Profit Margin Evaluation

Next, we move to the net profit margin. This margin is the remainder after deducting all your business expenses—not just the cost of goods sold but also overheads, taxes, and interest payments—from your revenue. This is often referred to as the bottom line and is a clear indicator of your overall business profitability.

Now, let's think about a creative agency. Their revenue comes from client projects. The direct costs might be the salaries of the designers and copywriters working on the project. But to calculate the net profit margin, they'd also need to consider indirect costs such as rent, administrative salaries, utilities, and marketing. By subtracting these costs from the revenue and expressing the result as a percentage of the revenue, they can determine their net profit margin.

I was taught a different approach to understanding profitability: view each expense as a direct deduction from your profit margin. Here's a clearer illustration: Suppose your business, with a revenue of one million dollars, operates at a 10% profit margin. This means that your profit is $100,000. Now, if you decide to spend $5,000 on a new expense, such as software or bonuses, you'll need an additional $50,000 in sales to compensate for this cost. Why? Because 10% of $50,000 equals $5,000, which is your expenditure. This perspective is crucial as it highlights how swiftly profits can diminish with new expenses, emphasizing the need for careful financial decision-making.

Return on Investment Calculation

Moving forward, it's time to consider your Return on Investment (ROI). ROI measures the efficiency of an investment and is used to compare the efficiency of different investments. In the business sphere, this could be related to any outflow of money related to business operations.

Imagine you run a gym and you've invested in a new type of workout machine. You're charging a premium for classes using this machine. To calculate the ROI, you'd subtract the cost of the machine from the net profit it generates, then divide this by the cost of the machine, and express it as a percentage. This gives you a reliable metric on the profitability of this investment.

Some of your potential business programs will present no immediate ROI. Organic marketing, SEO, and innovation are all commonly-referred to as categories with little observable ROI. Even such, investing in these expenses is a smart move that will eventually return your investment (hopefully exponentially, too).

Break-Even Analysis

Finally, let's conduct a break-even analysis. The break-even point is the point at which total revenue equals total costs, and your business is neither making a profit nor a loss. It's an essential tool for decision-making, planning, and controlling.

Let's say you run a coffee shop and you're considering introducing a new line of gourmet sandwiches. The break-even analysis will tell you how many sandwiches you need to sell to cover the costs associated with making and selling them, including ingredients, labor, and marketing. Anything above this number contributes to your net profit.

It's perfectly fine to be wrong, too. I've developed new lines of product or services that failed to deliver on their initial investment. Don't allow your concern for this risk to overtake your ability to take chances. Taking calculated risks is part of the entrepreneurial game.

In this part of your business journey, the focus is to ensure the profitability of your business. Each of these tools and metrics offer a different lens through which you can view your profitability. They're like navigational aids that help you steer your business towards financial success. As you move forward, keep your eyes on these indicators, adjusting your course as needed to stay on track towards your profitability goals.

With this solid foundation of financial understanding, you're well-equipped to take on the next chapter in your business adventure. The following chapter will delve into the human side of your business - hiring and team building. After all, a business is not just about numbers and margins; it's about people, too.

CHAPTER 2 - CHECKLIST

FINANCIAL SAVVY

- ☐ LEARN AN INCOME STATEMENT
- ☐ LEARN A BALANCE SHEET
- ☐ LEARN A CASH FLOW STATEMENT
- ☐ FORECAST REVENUE
- ☐ PLAN YOUR EXPENSES
- ☐ DEVELOP A CASH FLOW STRATEGY
- ☐ CONDUCT BREAK-EVEN ANALYSIS

CHAPTER 3:
THE PEOPLE FACTOR:
HIRING AND TEAM BUILDING

"When I find an employee who turns out to be wrong for a job, I feel it is my fault because I made the decision to hire him."
– Akio Morita

Imagine yourself as the conductor of an orchestra. Each musician plays a distinct role, each note contributing to the harmonious symphony that fills the air. But the music wouldn't exist without your skilled leadership, which is your ability to bring together diverse individuals and guide them towards a shared vision. This is the role you play as a business owner when it comes to hiring and building your team.

Like a beautiful symphony, a successful business is the result of various elements working in harmony. And at the heart of any thriving organization are its people. Selecting the right individuals to join your team, at the right time, is a critical aspect of leading a successful business. In this chapter, we'll explore this crucial process, starting with understanding the right time to hire.

3.1 WHEN TO HIRE: TIMING IS EVERYTHING

Business Growth Indicators

The decision to hire is often triggered by visible signs of business growth. These indicators could be an increase in sales, expanding customer base, or even the introduction of a new product or service line.

It's like noticing that your favorite indoor plant is outgrowing its pot. The leaves might be crowding each other out, or the roots might be jutting out of the drainage hole. These are clear signs that your plant needs more space to grow. Similarly, when your business starts to consistently hit or surpass its targets, it may indicate that it's time to expand your team.

Workload Assessment

Another critical factor to consider is workload. If you or your existing team are consistently overworked, it might be an indicator that you need to bring in additional hands.

Think about it like preparing a feast for a large gathering. You might be a fantastic cook, but trying to prepare multiple elaborate dishes single-handedly can be overwhelming. Sometimes, it's more efficient to rope in assistance so that you can focus on what you do best.

Evaluate the tasks being performed, the time it takes to complete them, and the impact on overall productivity and well-being. If critical tasks are being neglected or if there's a decline in service quality due to overwork, it might be time to hire.

Financial Capacity Evaluation

As crucial as it is to bring in help when the business is growing or the workload is increasing, it's equally important to consider your financial capacity. Hiring comes with financial implications - not just salaries, but also benefits, training, and other associated costs.

Consider this as planning a road trip. You wouldn't embark on a long journey without ensuring you have enough fuel to reach your destination. Similarly, before hiring, ensure your business has the financial fuel to sustain new additions to your team.

Review your financial statements, consider your projected income, and evaluate whether the increased productivity or sales from the new hire would justify the costs involved. If the numbers add up and the future looks promising, it might be time to expand your team.

Strategic Hiring Decisions

Lastly, strategic considerations can also play a role in deciding when to hire. You might need specific skills or expertise to implement your business strategy or to gain a competitive advantage.

Let's say you're planning to offer online ordering and delivery for your restaurant. You realize the potential increase in sales that this could bring, but you also recognize that you need someone with the right technical skills to manage this new service. In such a case, strategic hiring could be the key to unlocking this new growth opportunity.

In conclusion, hiring is a significant step in your business growth journey. It's about understanding the needs of your business, assessing your capacity, and making strategic decisions that align with your business goals. The decision to hire should not be taken lightly, but when timed correctly and done for the right reasons, it can be a game-changer for your business. After all, your team is your greatest asset, and investing in the right people can propel your business to new heights.

3.2 FINDING THE RIGHT PEOPLE

Job Description Development

The journey to finding the perfect candidate for your team begins with developing a comprehensive and well-thought-out job description. Consider this as the blueprint for your ideal employee – a document that not only outlines the specific role and responsibilities but also details the requisite skills and qualifications.

Crafting a job description is much like baking a cake. Each ingredient needs to be measured with precision and added in the right proportions. An excess or lack of any ingredient can alter the final outcome. In the same vein, your job description should strike a balance between outlining key responsibilities, desired skills, and the personal attributes that align with your company's core values, as established in Chapter 1. This is where you illustrate "what good looks like" in relation to these values.

For example, when hiring for a marketing position, the job description should clearly state the responsibilities involved, such as creating and executing marketing campaigns, managing social media accounts, and conducting market research. Furthermore, it should highlight essential skills including creativity, analytical ability, and strong communication capabilities.

This approach ensures that your job description not only attracts candidates with the necessary technical skills but also those who embody the values and culture of your organization. A well-crafted job description is a crucial step in the recruitment process, acting as a guide to identify candidates who are not just capable but also a perfect fit for your business ethos.

Effective Recruitment Strategies

With a well-defined job description in hand, the next step is to devise strategies to attract suitable candidates. This phase is like setting out a treasure map, which will guide potential candidates to discover the golden opportunity your business offers.

Your recruitment strategies could include posting on job portals, leveraging social networks, conducting job fairs, or even offering employee referral incentives. The choice of strategy would depend on the nature of the role and the type of candidates you wish to attract. Websites like Indeed, LinkedIn, and Glassdoor offer great opportunities to post jobs. Alternatively, you can find specialized websites like teamworkonline.com if you wish to post a role in the sports industry.

For instance, if you're recruiting for a tech role, you might consider reaching out to candidates through professional networking sites or tech forums. For a sales role, on the other hand, a job fair might be a more effective strategy.

Comprehensive Interview Process

Once you start receiving applications, the next phase is the interview process. This is where you get to interact with the candidates, assess their fit for the role, and evaluate their potential to contribute to your business.

The interview process is like a dance. It requires a rhythm, a sequence of steps designed to assess the candidate's skills, experience, and compatibility with your business culture.

Your interview process might include a preliminary screening round, one or more face-to-face interviews, and perhaps a practical task or assessment. Each step is designed to gather more information about the candidate, helping you form a holistic picture of their suitability for the role.

For a graphic designer role, for example, the practical task might involve creating a design based on a brief. For a customer service role, it could involve role-playing a customer interaction.

Candidate Evaluation and Selection

With the interviews completed, you enter the final stage of the hiring process - candidate evaluation and selection. This is the moment of truth, the point where you decide which candidate will join your team.

Evaluating candidates is akin to judging a talent show. You're not just looking for someone who can do the job. You're looking for a star performer, someone who can add value to your business and contribute to your team dynamics.

During the evaluation, you'll review the candidate's performance in the interview, their skills and qualifications, their potential for growth, and their fit with your business culture. You might also consider conducting reference checks to corroborate the information provided by the candidate.

Once you've made your decision, it's time to extend an offer to the chosen candidate. This is the beginning of a new chapter in your business story, a chapter that could be filled with growth, innovation, and success with the right people on your team.

3.3 BUILDING A HIGH-PERFORMING TEAM

The Org Chart

The foundation for building a high-performing team begins with the development of an Organizational Chart (Org Chart). This tool is indispensable in mapping out the structure of your team, hence, providing a clear visual representation of how each role interconnects within the organization. More than just a diagram, an Org Chart is instrumental in highlighting the existing framework of your team and pinpointing any vacancies or structural gaps. This level of clarity is crucial for effectively planning future recruitment and understanding which roles need to be filled next.

While there are various **HR** software tools, commonly referred to as Human Resources Information Systems (HRIS), that offer functionalities to create an Org Chart, certain platforms stand out for their user-friendliness and efficiency. One such recommendation is Organimi.com, known for its robust and intuitive org chart program. Utilizing a tool like Organimi.com simplifies the process of chart creation and management, making it easier to maintain an up-to-date and accurate reflection of your team's structure.

In essence, an Org Chart is more than just an organizational tool; it's a strategic instrument that aids in the visualization and optimization of your team's composition. It serves as a roadmap for both current and future staffing needs, ensuring that your team's structure aligns with your business objectives and facilitates the creation of a cohesive and high-performing team.

Team Role Definition

Picture a well-oiled machine. Each cog, each gear, each component has a specific role to play. Together, in perfect synchronization, they bring the machine to life. A high-performing team operates in much the same way. Each member has a defined role, and each role contributes to the team's collective goals.

Defining team roles isn't merely about assigning tasks or job titles. Instead, it's about understanding each individual's strengths, weaknesses, and interests, and aligning these with the needs of your business. It's about creating a space where everyone knows what they're doing, why they're doing it, and how it contributes to the bigger picture.

Take, for instance, a software development team. You have developers, testers, UX designers, and project managers. Each role is distinct, but they're all intertwined, working towards the common goal of creating a superior product.

Team Building Activities

Now, let's think of a garden. A variety of plants, each with its unique characteristics, together create a vibrant and beautiful landscape. But these plants didn't just sprout overnight. They were nurtured, cared for, and encouraged to grow. Similarly, a high-performing team isn't formed overnight. It's built through shared experiences, mutual trust, and a sense of camaraderie.

Team building activities are a powerful tool in this regard. They're not just about fun and games; they're about fostering relationships, improving communication, and cultivating a collaborative spirit.

For instance, a team cooking challenge doesn't just test culinary skills, it also enhances teamwork, problem-solving, and leadership skills. A group volunteering event, on the other hand, can foster empathy, social responsibility, and a sense of shared purpose.

Performance Management

Performance management in a business setting is akin to how sports coaches nurture and develop their team. It's not just about giving instructions or waiting for the year-end review; it's a dynamic, ongoing process that's integral to building a high-performing team.

Effective performance management is continuous and multifaceted. It involves regularly setting clear expectations, tracking progress, providing timely feedback, addressing challenges, and celebrating achievements. This approach ensures that team members are always aligned with the company's goals and have the support they need to meet them.

Regular coaching sessions are key. I recommend weekly one-on-ones (1:1s) with direct reports. These meetings are opportunities for honest, transparent conversations about performance, goals, challenges, and professional development. They also help in building trust and understanding between the manager and the team member, thereby fostering a positive work environment.

Additionally, detailed quarterly reviews are essential. These should comprehensively cover the past quarter's results, providing a broader perspective on the employee's performance. This is not just about assessing what has been achieved but also about understanding how it was achieved and setting the stage for future goals.

For example, a sales manager could establish monthly sales targets and then, in weekly 1:1s, discuss progress, tackle any hurdles, offer strategic coaching, and give recognition where necessary. Celebrating successes, whether big or small, motivates the team and reinforces positive behaviors.

The concept of 'failing fast' with new hires is also an important aspect of performance management. It's about taking calculated risks in hiring, being observant, and making swift, informed decisions. If a new hire isn't meeting expectations despite support and guidance, it's crucial to acknowledge this and take appropriate action. This could mean additional training, reassignment, or, if necessary, ending their tenure. The goal is to ensure the right fit for both the employee and the team, maintaining the overall effectiveness and morale.

In summary, performance management is a vital tool for any leader. It's about creating a culture where continuous improvement is encouraged, where feedback is constructive, and where successes are celebrated. This approach not only drives performance but also nurtures a committed and engaged workforce.

Employee Motivation Techniques

Lastly, we come to employee motivation. Think of it as the fuel that powers your team. Without it, even the most skilled and talented individuals can fail to reach their potential.

Motivating your team is about more than just financial incentives. It's about creating an environment where people feel valued, engaged, and inspired.

This could involve providing opportunities for learning and growth, recognizing and rewarding effort, creating a positive work culture, or even something as simple as a thank you note for a job well done.

For instance, a customer service manager might motivate their team by recognizing excellent customer feedback, providing training for skill development, or organizing regular team lunches to build camaraderie.

Building a high-performing team is a dynamic and ongoing process. It requires clear role definition, team building activities, performance management, and motivation techniques. With these elements in place, you can create a team that's not just productive and efficient, but also engaged, committed, and ready to propel your business towards its goals.

3.4 EFFECTIVE TEAM COMMUNICATION

Open Communication Culture

Imagine a bustling marketplace filled with vendors and patrons. The air is charged with energy, punctuated by the rhythmic cadence of bargaining, the exchange of ideas, the sharing of stories. This dynamic environment thrives on open communication. In much the same way, your team needs a culture of open communication to thrive.

Creating an open communication culture is about fostering an environment where ideas and opinions can be freely shared without fear of judgment or reprisal. It's about encouraging dialogue, promoting transparency, and valuing diversity of thought.

Picture a software development team brainstorming ideas for a new feature. In an open communication culture, every team member, regardless of their role or seniority, feels comfortable sharing their ideas, knowing they'll be heard and respected. This kind of inclusive brainstorming can spark innovative solutions and foster collaborative problem-solving.

Communication Tools

The aspiration to foster open communication within a business is laudable. However, achieving this goal effectively hinges on utilizing the right communication tools. These tools act as the lifeline of your team, offering a centralized platform for interaction and information sharing. Selecting the most suitable tool for your team depends on a variety of factors such as the size of your business, the nature of your operations, and whether your team members work remotely.

Among the plethora of options available, Slack often stands out due to its versatility and user-friendly interface. However, it's important to explore other viable alternatives that might better suit your specific business needs. Microsoft Teams, Basecamp, Google Chat, and Discord are all commendable choices, each with its unique set of features tailored to different operational requirements.

In an era where digital communication is paramount, the importance of choosing an apt communication tool cannot be overstated. It is not merely a matter of convenience but a critical component in fostering a cohesive and effective team dynamic. The ideal tool should not only facilitate seamless communication but also enhances collaboration, streamline your team's workflow, and nurture a connected, engaged, and productive work environment. By carefully selecting and implementing the right communication tool, you lay the groundwork for a more synchronized, transparent, and efficient team, hence, propelling your business towards greater success.

Regular Team Meetings

Now, let's consider the role of regular team meetings. Picture a sports team huddling together before a game, discussing strategies, setting expectations, and boosting morale. This huddle isn't just a ritual; it's a crucial strategy for aligning the team and fostering unity.

In the business context, regular team meetings serve a similar purpose. They provide a platform for sharing updates, discussing challenges, brainstorming solutions, and recognizing achievements. They keep everyone on the same page and foster a sense of collective purpose.

For instance, a marketing team might hold weekly meetings to review campaign progress, discuss upcoming projects, share market insights, and celebrate wins. These meetings not only facilitate information sharing, but also builds team cohesion and spirit.

Establishing a regular meeting cadence is not only crucial but will become a consistent practice your team would follow each week. Regarding meeting duration, I suggest adhering to these guidelines: Limit meetings focused on specific problems or tasks to between 30 and 60 minutes. Weekly team meetings should last between 30 and 90 minutes, which would vary based on team size and the agenda.

It's vital to establish this rhythm and ensure that your team adheres to these principles. Excessive meetings can be detrimental to a small team's productivity. However, avoiding meetings entirely can also be counterproductive, as it may lead to a lack of team engagement and a sense of disconnect from the business. Finding the right balance is key. Experiment to discover the meeting cadence that works best for your business.

Constructive Feedback Mechanisms

Think of a skilled craftsman shaping a piece of metal into a beautiful piece of jewelry. He doesn't just hammer away at it indiscriminately; he applies precise, deliberate strokes, constantly assessing and adjusting his technique to achieve the desired shape. Providing feedback to your team members requires a similar level of care and precision.

Constructive feedback mechanisms are about providing clear, specific, and actionable feedback that helps team members understand what they're doing well and where they can improve. It's about focusing on the behavior, not the person, and delivering the feedback in a manner that's respectful and encouraging.

Imagine a sales manager providing feedback to a team member after a client's presentation. The manager praises the team member's thorough research and clear communication but suggests that they could engage the client more effectively by asking probing questions. This kind of constructive feedback can boost performance and drive professional growth.

Feedback Loops

Incorporating effective feedback loops is a vital aspect of establishing robust communication standards within your company. Feedback loops are structured systems or processes that facilitate a two-way flow of feedback between you and your team. They are essential for providing a platform where both leadership and team members can openly express their opinions, concerns, and suggestions. This reciprocal communication is key to addressing any areas of dissatisfaction and collaboratively discussing business plans and strategies.

To cultivate a culture of open feedback, I recommend implementing tools such as the quarterly Employee Net

Promoter Score (eNPS) survey. This survey should be designed to elicit responses on aspects critical to the business while also giving employees the opportunity to offer candid, anonymous feedback. Actively responding to this feedback, by communicating and implementing plans to address any concerns raised, is instrumental in building trust and respect within your team.

However, relying solely on quarterly surveys for feedback may not suffice for maintaining a continuous loop of communication. It's imperative to complement these surveys with more frequent interactions, such as weekly or bi-weekly one-on-one meetings (1:1s) with your direct reports. These 1:1s serve as a platform for team members to voice their opinions about your performance, the business's direction, and any other pertinent issues. Encouraging regular, open dialogues like these not only ensures that feedback is timely and relevant but also fosters a sense of inclusivity and value among team members, ultimately contributing to the ongoing improvement and success of the business.

Conflict Resolution Strategies

Finally, let's address the proverbial elephant in the room - conflict. Like a storm on the horizon, conflict is often seen as a threatening force, something to be avoided at all costs. But when handled effectively, conflict can be a catalyst for growth, sparking new ideas, challenging assumptions, and strengthening relationships.

Effective conflict resolution strategies involve acknowledging the conflict, understanding the perspectives of those involved, facilitating a constructive dialogue to find a solution, and fostering reconciliation. It's about turning the storm of conflict into a rainbow of understanding and cooperation.

For example, consider a design team where two members have a disagreement over the color scheme for a project. A constructive conflict resolution approach might involve understanding each person's perspective, facilitating a discussion to explore different options, and finding a mutually agreeable solution. Through this process, the team members not only resolve their conflict but also learn to collaborate more effectively.

In conclusion, effective team communication is a vital ingredient in the recipe for a successful business. It's about creating an open communication culture, holding regular team meetings, implementing constructive feedback mechanisms like feedback loops, and employing effective conflict resolution strategies. With these elements in place, you're well on your way to nurturing a high-performing team that can take your business to new heights.

We've covered a lot of ground in this chapter- from hiring the right people to building a strong team. However, leading a team isn't just about managing others; it's also about managing yourself. In the next chapter, we'll explore the art of leadership in small business, thereby, equipping you with the tools and insights you need to lead your team with confidence and competence.

THE PEOPLE FACTOR

- ☐ **ASSESS BUSINESS GROWTH**
- ☐ **DEVELOP JOB DESCRIPTIONS**
- ☐ **BUILD INTERVIEW PROCESS**
- ☐ **ESTABLISH ROLES & ORG CHART**
- ☐ **CREATE FEEDBACK LOOP**
- ☐ **DEVELOP MEETING CADENCE**
- ☐ **SET COMMUNICATION TOOLS**

CHAPTER 4:
THE ART OF LEADERSHIP IN SMALL BUSINESS

"The best executive is the one who has sense enough to pick good men to do what he wants done, and self-restraint enough to keep from meddling with them while they do it."
– Theodore Roosevelt

Imagine standing at the helm of a ship, gazing out over the vast sea. The wind is in your hair, the salt air in your lungs, and the power of leadership in your hands. As the captain, you hold the course of your vessel, guiding it through calm seas and stormy waters alike. This is your role as a small business owner - a leader navigating the exciting seas of entrepreneurship.

The leadership style you choose to adopt can significantly impact your business, affecting everything from company culture to business performance. Let's explore different leadership styles and their potential impact on your business.

4.1 LEADERSHIP STYLES AND THEIR IMPACT

Transformational Leadership

Think back to a time when you encountered a leader who inspired you, who challenged you to think differently, and who propelled you to exceed your own expectations. That's transformational leadership in action.

Transformational leaders inspire their teams with a shared vision, fostering an environment of trust and respect. They encourage creativity, value individual strengths, and motivate team members to strive for excellence. In your small business, adopting a transformational leadership style can lead to increased productivity, higher employee satisfaction, and enhanced team performance.

Autocratic Leadership

Picture a seasoned chef in a bustling kitchen, directing each step of a complex recipe with precision and control. That's an example of autocratic leadership - a style characterized by individual control over all decisions, with minimal input from team members.

In your business, autocratic leadership might be useful in situations that require quick decision-making, clear direction, or strict control. However, overuse of this style can stifle creativity and demotivate your team, leading to lower job satisfaction and higher employee turnover.

Laissez-faire Leadership

Imagine a free-flowing jazz band, where each musician is given the freedom to express their unique style, contributing to a harmonious yet dynamic performance. This is the essence of laissez-faire leadership, a style where leaders provide minimal direction and maximum freedom to their team.

In your business, laissez-faire leadership can foster innovation, creativity, and job satisfaction, especially in a team of highly skilled and self-motivated individuals. However, without clear direction and control, this style can also lead to poor performance and lack of progress.

Democratic Leadership

Visualize a round-table discussion, where each participant's opinion is valued, and decisions are made collectively. This is democratic leadership, a style characterized by shared decision-making and active participation of team members.

In your business, democratic leadership can foster a sense of ownership, boost team morale, and encourage diverse perspectives, leading to better decision-making. However, this style may also lead to slower decision-making and potential conflicts, especially in a team with diverse viewpoints.

Transactional Leadership

Think of a classic customer-service scenario, where the employee knows that if they meet their targets, they'll receive a bonus. This is transactional leadership in action - a style based on a system of rewards and punishments.

In your business, transactional leadership can be effective in driving specific behaviors and achieving set goals, especially for routine or unskilled tasks. However, over-reliance on this style can limit your team's creativity and reduce their intrinsic motivation.

Each leadership style has its strengths and weaknesses, and the impact on your business can vary depending on the context. The secret lies in understanding these styles and adapting your leadership approach based on the situation, your team's needs, and your business goals. Remember, as the captain of your entrepreneurial ship, your leadership style sets the course for your business's journey. Choose wisely, and you'll navigate your team towards success.

4.2 DECISION MAKING AND DELEGATION

Steps for Effective Decision Making

Envision yourself as a seasoned explorer in a dense forest, standing at a crossroads. Each path leading to a different destination, each choice carrying its own set of potential outcomes. This, in essence, mirrors the process of decision making in business leadership.

The first step in effective decision making is to clearly define the problem or decision at hand. Perhaps you need to decide whether to launch a new product or identify ways to improve team productivity.

Next, gather all necessary information related to the decision. This could involve market research, financial analysis, or team feedback, among other things. Using our explorer analogy, this would be like studying the terrain, considering the weather, and assessing your resources before choosing a path.

The third step is to evaluate the options. Each decision usually comes with a set of alternatives. Weigh the pros and cons of each option, considering factors such as cost, time, resources, and alignment with your business goals.

Once you've evaluated the alternatives, make your decision. Choose the option that offers the best solution to the problem or decision at hand.

Finally, implement the decision and monitor the results. This allows you to assess the effectiveness of your decision and make necessary adjustments moving forward.

Importance of Delegation

Imagine a skilled magician performing a complex illusion. To the audience, it appears as if they're single-handedly creating the magic. But behind the scenes, a well-coordinated team supports the magician, each contributing to the success of the illusion. This is the power of delegation in leadership.

Delegation is the act of entrusting tasks and responsibilities to your team members. It's not about offloading work; it's about empowering your team, optimizing productivity, and focusing your efforts where they're needed most.

In the realm of small business, where resources are often limited, effective delegation is critical. It allows you to make the most of your team's skills and strengths, fosters a sense of responsibility among your team members, and frees up your time to focus on strategic decision-making and leadership duties.

Strategies for Successful Delegation

Crafting a masterpiece requires more than just quality paints and brushes; it requires an artist who knows how to blend colors, choose the right brush strokes, and bring their vision to life. Similarly, successful delegation requires more than just assigning tasks; it requires thoughtfulness, trust, and effective communication.

Start by selecting the right person for the task. Then, consider their skills, interests, and workload. Assigning a task to someone who lacks the necessary skills or is already overloaded can lead to poor results and decreased morale.

Once you've identified the right person, clearly communicate the task. Ensure they understand what's expected, why it's important, and how it fits into the larger picture.

Provide the necessary authority and resources to complete the task. This might include access to specific tools, approval authorities, or input from other team members.

Finally, establish a system for feedback and follow-up. This enables you to track progress, provide support, and acknowledge achievements, fostering a positive delegation experience for both you and your team member.

Overcoming Delegation Challenges

Navigating a ship through a storm requires skill, courage, and perseverance. Similarly, overcoming delegation challenges requires understanding, flexibility, and determination.

One common challenge is the fear of losing control. It's natural to feel apprehensive about handing over tasks, especially if you're used to doing everything yourself. Overcoming this fear requires trust in your team's abilities and accepting that different doesn't necessarily mean worse.

Another challenge is unclear communication. If team members are unsure about what's expected, they're likely to make mistakes. To avoid this, ensure you communicate tasks clearly and provide opportunities for questions and clarification.

Balancing delegation with workload is another common challenge. It's important to delegate tasks equitably and consider each team member's capacity and capabilities.

Finally, remember that delegation is not a one-way street. Be open to feedback from your team about the delegation process. Their insights can help you refine your approach and become a more effective leader.

4.3 CONFLICT RESOLUTION STRATEGIES

Active Listening

Imagine standing in the middle of a bustling city, taking in the symphony of sounds. The distant hum of traffic, the rhythmic tap of a pedestrian's footsteps, the soft rustle of leaves in the breeze. Amidst this cacophony, you tune your ears to a familiar melody, a favorite song playing in a nearby café. This is the essence of active listening, the ability to tune out distractions and focus on the matter at hand.

Active listening is not merely about hearing the words that are spoken, but understanding the emotions, intentions, and implications behind them. It involves maintaining eye contact, using body language to show engagement, and providing verbal feedback to convey understanding.

In the context of conflict resolution, active listening allows you to understand each party's perspective and validate their feelings, fostering mutual respect and open communication. This sets the stage for a constructive dialogue, moving you one step closer to resolving the conflict.

Mediation Techniques

Consider a skilled referee during a heated football match. Their role is not to play the game or take sides, but to facilitate fair play and ensure that the rules are followed. In the realm of conflict resolution, the role of a mediator is much the same.

Mediation involves facilitating a discussion between the conflicting parties, helping them express their views, understand each other's perspective, and work towards a mutually acceptable solution. It's not about dictating an outcome, but guiding the parties involved toward finding their own resolution.

The mediator's role is to ensure that the conversation remains focused, respectful, and productive. They might use techniques such as reframing negative statements into positive ones, encouraging empathy, and guiding the conversation towards problem-solving, rather than blaming.

Problem-Solving Approach

Picture a complex puzzle- a jumble of pieces waiting to be assembled into a coherent image. The solution doesn't lie in focusing on one piece alone but in understanding how the pieces fit together. Similarly, a problem-solving approach to conflict resolution involves understanding the bigger picture and finding a solution that addresses the root cause of the conflict.

The problem-solving process begins with defining the problem. This involves understanding the underlying issues that have led to the conflict. Next, generate potential solutions. Encourage all parties to contribute ideas, fostering collaboration and buy-in.

Once you've brainstormed solutions, evaluate each one. Discuss the pros and cons and consider the feasibility of implementation. Finally, agree on a solution. Ensure that all parties are satisfied with the chosen solution and commit to implementing it.

Negotiation Skills

Imagine a bustling market, where buyers and sellers haggle over prices, each aiming to strike a deal that suits their interests. This negotiation dance is not just about getting the best price; it's about finding a balance between what the buyer is willing to pay and what the seller is willing to accept. This delicate balance is the cornerstone of negotiation skills in conflict resolution.

Negotiation is not about winning or losing; it's about finding a win-win solution that satisfies all parties involved. It involves understanding each party's interests, exploring creative options, and seeking fair outcomes.

Effective negotiation skills include the ability to communicate clearly, listen actively, think critically, and make decisions collaboratively. It also requires patience, empathy, and the ability to manage emotions, both yours and others.

In the face of conflict, it's easy to let emotions take the driver's seat. But with these conflict resolution strategies at your disposal, you're equipped to navigate through the storm with grace and poise. Remember, conflicts are not roadblocks on your path to success, but stepping stones. They offer opportunities for growth, learning, and strengthening relationships. So, embrace them, learn from them, and let them guide you towards becoming a better leader.

4.4 FOSTERING A POSITIVE COMPANY CULTURE

Importance of Core Values

Imagine a sturdy tree, standing tall and firm in the face of a raging storm. Its strength lies not in its branches or leaves, but in its root that anchors it to the ground. For your business, these roots are your core values - the principles that underpin your organization and guide its growth.

Core values serve as the moral compass of your company, guiding decision-making, shaping behavior, and defining your identity. They are the essence of your company's identity - the principles, beliefs, or philosophy of values.

For instance, if one of your core values is integrity, it should be reflected in all aspects of your business - from transparent communication with your team to honest dealings with your customers. It's not just about stating these values; it's about living them every day.

It's crucial to clearly define your core values and make them visible to your entire team. Regularly recognizing and rewarding team members who exemplify these values not only sets a standard for what excellence looks like but also helps in cultivating a culture that's truly aligned with these principles. Such acknowledgment serves as a powerful tool in reinforcing these core values and fostering an environment where they are lived out daily.

The Role of Communication

Just like a group of skilled musicians who, despite their individual talents, create the most enchanting music only when they play in perfect harmony, effective communication in a business environment is what transforms a group of individuals into a high-functioning, cohesive team.

In the realm of business, communication is akin to the lifeblood that keeps various parts of the organization interconnected and functioning smoothly. It's the channel through which your vision is shared, expectations are set, feedback is delivered, and a culture of transparency and trust is nurtured. Effective communication isn't limited to just the content of the message; it encompasses how the message is conveyed and the importance of active listening.

Setting clear expectations is a critical component of communication. It involves articulating what is required from each team member, thereby eliminating ambiguities and setting the stage for accountability and alignment with the company's objectives. When expectations are clearly communicated, team members have a precise understanding of their roles, responsibilities, and the standards against which their performance will be evaluated. This clarity not only aids in effective task execution but also contributes to a more harmonious and productive work environment.

Implementing regular team meetings, maintaining open-door policies, and utilizing collaborative tools are practical ways to foster open and effective communication. These practices encourage the free flow of information and ideas, ensuring that every team member feels involved and informed. It's crucial to remember that communication is a two-way street; it's as much about listening to and understanding the perspectives and concerns of your team as it is about conveying your own thoughts and directives.

For instance, in team meetings, it's not just about disseminating information, it's also about inviting feedback, encouraging dialogue, and genuinely considering the input of team members. An open-door policy enhances accessibility and fosters a culture where team members feel valued and comfortable sharing their ideas and concerns.

In essence, the role of communication in a business setting is multifaceted and indispensable. By prioritizing clear, consistent, and bidirectional communication, you lay the foundation for a team that operates not just with efficiency but with harmony and shared purpose, much like a beautifully orchestrated symphony.

Employee Engagement Strategies

Think of a bustling beehive, buzzing with activity. Each bee plays a critical role, working diligently for the betterment of the hive. This level of engagement doesn't happen by chance; it's the result of a supportive environment, clear roles, and a shared purpose. Similarly, fostering employee engagement in your business requires deliberate effort and strategic planning.

Employee engagement is about creating a workplace where employees feel passionate about their work, committed to the organization, and put discretionary effort into their work. It's about going the extra mile, not because they have to, but because they want to.

Strategies to foster employee engagement could include providing opportunities for professional growth, aligning individual roles with company goals, and creating a positive work environment. When employees are engaged, they're more productive, more loyal, and more likely to go above and beyond to contribute to the company's success.

Recognition and Reward Systems

Picture a runner crossing the finish line after a grueling race. The medal they receive is not just a piece of metal; it's a symbol of their hard work, determination, and achievement. In the same vein, recognition and reward systems in your business are not just about giving out bonuses or awards; they're about acknowledging effort, appreciating contribution, and celebrating success.

Recognition is about expressing appreciation for an employee's work. It's about noticing the effort of your employees and acknowledging it in a meaningful way. This could be a simple thank you note, a shout-out in a team meeting, or a certificate of achievement.

On the other hand, rewards are tangible expressions of appreciation. They could take the form of bonuses, gift cards, extra time off, or any other perk that would hold value for the employee.

When employees feel recognized and rewarded, they're more motivated, more engaged, and are more likely to stay with your company.

In a world where businesses are often judged solely on their products or profits, a positive company culture can be a powerful differentiator. It's the heart of your business- pumping energy, inspiration, and morale through every part of your organization. So, invest in your culture, nurture it, and watch as it breathes life into your business, creating an environment where success is not just possible but inevitable. As we move forward on this exciting path of entrepreneurship, we'll explore how to market your business effectively, attract customers and drive growth.

THE ART OF LEADERSHIP

- [ ] IDENTIFY YOUR LEADERSHIP STYLE
- [ ] LEARN DECISION MAKING SKILLS
- [ ] PRACTICE DELEGATION
- [ ] PRACTICE ACTIVE LISTENING
- [ ] LEARN ABOUT NEGOTIATION
- [ ] DRAFT CORE VALUES DOCUMENT
- [ ] SET RECOGNITION & REWARDS PLAN

CHAPTER 5:
MARKETING YOUR BUSINESS: THE CUSTOMER-CENTRIC APPROACH

"I've learned that people will forget what you said, people will forget what you did, but people will never forget how you made them feel."
— Maya Angelou

Imagine you're hosting a dinner party. As a thoughtful host, you would likely put some effort into understanding your guests' preferences. You would think about their dietary restrictions, their favorite cuisines, and perhaps even their preferred dining ambiance. This thoughtful approach guarantees that your guests feel valued, their needs met, and they have an enjoyable experience at your party. In a similar vein, understanding your customers is the first step to effective marketing in your business. Let's explore this further.

5.1 UNDERSTANDING YOUR CUSTOMER

Understanding your customer is akin to understanding the rules of a game. Just as each game has its unique set of rules, each customer segment has its unique needs, preferences, and behaviors. By gaining a deep understanding of your customers, you can tailor your products, services, and marketing strategies to meet their needs effectively.

Customer Segmentation

Think of your customer base as a puzzle. Each customer is a unique piece, and customer segmentation is the process of fitting these pieces together to form a complete picture. It involves dividing your customers into distinct groups based on common characteristics such as age, gender, income, buying behavior, and more.

For instance, if you're running a fitness center, one segment might be for young professionals looking for high-intensity workouts, while another could be for seniors seeking low-impact exercise classes. By segmenting your customers, you can tailor your offerings and marketing messages to each group, ensuring they resonate with your customers' specific needs and interests.

Customer Needs Analysis

Now that you've segmented your customers, the next step is to understand their needs. This involves digging deeper to understand what your customers are looking for, what problems they are facing, and how your product or service can provide a solution.

Using the fitness center example, the young professionals might need flexible timings to accommodate their busy schedules, while the seniors might need personalized guidance to exercise safely. By conducting a thorough needs analysis, you can identify these specific requirements and tailor your services accordingly.

Customer Behavior Patterns

Understanding customer behavior patterns is like reading a book. Each behavior tells a story, revealing insights about the customer's preferences, habits, and decision-making process.

For instance, you might notice that the young professionals in your fitness center prefer attending evening classes, while the seniors prefer morning sessions. You might also observe that some customers are regular attendees, while others drop in occasionally. These behavior patterns can inform your scheduling, pricing, and customer engagement strategies.

Customer Feedback Mechanisms

Finally, establish mechanisms to collect customer feedback. This is like a suggestion box at your dinner party, providing a platform for your guests to share their thoughts, experiences, and suggestions. These feedback loops are identical to what you are building within your internal team.

In your business, this could take the form of surveys, feedback forms, social media interactions, or even informal conversations. Feedback mechanisms not only provide valuable insights into your customers' needs and experiences but also make your customers feel valued and heard.

In conclusion, understanding your customer is the cornerstone of effective marketing. It's about seeing the world from your customers' perspective, understanding their needs and behaviors, and using these insights to shape your business offerings and marketing strategies. Remember, in the game of business, the customer is the queen or king, and understanding them is your winning move.

As we move forward in this chapter, we'll explore how to leverage your understanding of your customers to build a strong brand, develop effective marketing strategies, and harness the power of social media to grow your business. So, put on your marketing hat and get ready to dive into the exciting world of customer-centric marketing.

5.2 BUILDING A STRONG BRAND

Brand Identity Development

Consider a beacon, steadfast and unmistakable, guiding lost ships to safety. Your brand identity serves a similar purpose; it sets you apart in a sea of competitors and draws your target customers towards you. Crafting your brand identity should be a thoughtful and intentional process. It's about defining your brand's essence - its personality, values, and visual elements that make it instantly recognizable.

Think of a popular soft drink brand, the first things that come to mind might be its iconic logo, its distinctive red and white color scheme, and its tagline. These elements, together, form its brand identity. For your business, developing a strong brand identity could involve creating a unique logo, selecting specific colors or fonts, or crafting a catchy slogan.

Brand Positioning Strategies

Next, consider a game of chess. You strategically place your pieces to control key positions on the board. Similarly, brand positioning involves strategically placing your brand in the minds of your customers. It's about defining how your brand is different from your competitors and why your target customers should choose you over them.

For example, a family-run restaurant might position itself as a provider of home-cooked meals made with locally sourced ingredients, differentiating itself from fast-food chains. To develop effective brand positioning strategies for your business, consider what sets you apart from your competitors, what your customers value about your product or service, and how you can communicate this value proposition to your target audience.

Brand Messaging

Imagine a drumbeat, setting the rhythm for a song. Consistent and clear, it gives the song its pulse. Your brand messaging serves a similar purpose; it sets the tone for your brand communications, providing a consistent and clear message about your brand's value.

Your brand messaging should be a reflection of your brand identity and positioning. It's about communicating your unique value proposition, your brand's personality, and its promise to your customers.

For instance, a tech startup might have brand a messaging that emphasizes innovation, user-friendliness, and superior customer support. To create effective brand messaging for your business, consider what your brand stands for, what promise you're making to your customers, and how you can communicate this in a way that resonates with your target audience.

Branding Consistency

Finally, consider a familiar melody. Even if played on different instruments or in different styles, the melody remains recognizable because of its consistent pattern. Similarly, branding consistency is about ensuring that your brand identity, positioning, and messaging remain consistent across all touchpoints.

Branding consistency reinforces brand recognition, builds trust with your customers, and enhances your brand equity. For example, a luxury fashion brand would maintain consistency by using the same logo, color scheme, and tone of voice across its website, social media, and print advertising.

To maintain branding consistency in your business, establish brand guidelines that outline how your brand elements should be used. Regularly review your brand touchpoints to ensure adherence to these guidelines.

Remember, building a strong brand is not a one-off task; it's an ongoing process that requires consistency, creativity, and strategic thinking. But the payoff is worth it. A strong brand can set you apart from your competitors, attract and retain customers, and drive business growth. So, invest in your brand, nurture it, and watch as it shines brightly in the marketplace, drawing customers towards your business like a beacon on a dark night.

5.3 EFFECTIVE MARKETING STRATEGIES

Content Marketing

Imagine a bustling library, shelves lined with books, each one offering a unique story, a different perspective. This is the essence of content marketing. It's about creating and sharing valuable content to attract and engage your target audience, and ultimately, drive profitable customer action.

The 'content' in content marketing could take many forms - blog posts, videos, podcasts, infographics, and more. The key is to ensure that the content is valuable, relevant, and consistent.

For instance, if you run a travel agency, your content could include blog posts about travel tips, videos showcasing exotic destinations, or infographics about the best times to visit certain locations. This content not only attracts potential customers but also positions your brand as a trusted resource in the travel industry.

Email Marketing

Think of email marketing as sending a personalized invitation to a party. It's a direct and personalized way to communicate with your target audience, building relationships and promoting your products or services.

Effective email marketing involves crafting compelling subject lines, creating engaging content, and including clear calls to action. It also involves segmenting your email list to deliver tailored messages to different customer groups.

For example, a boutique clothing store might send an email to their customers showcasing their new summer collection, with a special discount code for loyal customers. This not only promotes the new collection but also rewards customer loyalty, creating a win-win situation.

SEO and SEM

Imagine you're on a treasure hunt, searching for a hidden treasure based on clues and a map. In the world of digital marketing, that treasure is high search engine ranking, and the clues and map are Search Engine Optimization (SEO) and Search Engine Marketing (SEM).

SEO involves optimizing your website and content to achieve higher rankings in search engine results, making it easier for potential customers to find you. This could involve keyword optimization, link building, and ensuring a mobile-friendly website design.

SEM, on the other hand, involves promoting your website through paid advertising on search engines. This can help you gain visibility in search engine results, driving more traffic to your website.

For instance, a local bakery might use SEO strategies to rank higher for search terms like 'fresh bread in [city name]' and use

SEM to run targeted ad campaigns during the holiday season, attracting customers looking for holiday treats.

Influencer Marketing

Consider the impact of a popular celebrity wearing a new fashion brand at a high-profile event. Suddenly, the brand becomes a household name, and sales skyrocket. This is the power of influencer marketing.

Influencer marketing involves collaborating with influential individuals, usually on social media, to promote your brand or product. The key is to partner with influencers who align with your brand values and have a following that matches your target audience.

For example, a skincare brand might partner with a beauty influencer to create a video tutorial featuring their products. The influencer's endorsement serves as a powerful testimonial, driving their followers to try the products for themselves.

Offline Marketing

While digital marketing offers many benefits, let's not forget the power of offline marketing. Think of offline marketing as a handshake - it's personal, direct, and leaves a lasting impression.

Offline marketing can take various forms, including print advertising, direct mail, networking events, sponsorships, and more. It's all about creating tangible touchpoints that connect your brand with your target audience in the physical world.

For instance, a restaurant might distribute flyers in the local neighborhood offering a discount on first-time orders. They might also sponsor a local community event and serve samples of their signature dishes. These offline marketing efforts not only raise brand awareness but also builds community goodwill.

Marketing, in its essence, is a conversation between your brand and your customers. It's about understanding your customers' needs, offering valuable solutions, and building relationships. By exploring a mix of different marketing strategies, both online and offline, you can create a marketing mix that resonates with your target audience, amplifies your brand, and drives business growth. So, get creative, experiment with different strategies, and find the mix that works best for your business.

5.4 SOCIAL MEDIA AND YOUR BUSINESS

Imagine yourself at a buzzing networking event. You're there to meet new people, share ideas, and promote your business. In the digital landscape, social media platforms serve a similar purpose. They're vibrant online networking hubs where you can connect with your audience, showcase your brand, and expand your reach. But just like at a networking event, your success on social media hinges on your approach. Let's dive into it.

Choosing the Right Platforms

Think about the networking event again. You wouldn't go to a tech startup event if you were looking to connect with artisan bakers, right? Similarly, choosing the right social media platform depends on your target audience. Each platform has its own unique user demographics and characteristics.

Facebook, with its diverse user base, might be great for a family-run restaurant aiming to connect with local customers. LinkedIn, with its professional focus, could be ideal for a B2B software firm looking to reach decision-makers in specific industries. Instagram, with its visual nature, might be perfect for a fashion brand targeting millennials. The key lies in understanding where your audience spends their time online and focusing your efforts on those platforms.

Social Media Content Planning

Making a valuable contribution at a networking event requires thoughtful preparation. You need a game plan on what insights to share, questions to ask, and how to present your business. In the social media world, this is akin to content planning.

Content planning involves deciding what type of content to share (such as photos, videos, articles), when to share it, and how it aligns with your overall marketing goals. A pet store might share cute pet photos, tips on pet care, customer testimonials, and promotional offers. Ensuring a mix of informative, entertaining, and promotional content can keep your audience engaged and reinforce your brand image.

Social Media Advertising

At a networking event, you might sponsor a presentation or a refreshment break to increase your visibility. On social media, paid advertising serves a similar purpose, as it allows you to extend your reach, target specific audience groups, and gain more visibility.

In the review phase, it's important to explore the various networking groups available in your business sector. This could mean becoming a member of your local Chamber of Commerce or joining a city-based business mastermind group. The goal is to research the options out there and determine which group aligns best with your needs and objectives.

Social media advertising can be highly targeted, as it allows you to reach people based on their demographics, interests, behaviors, and more. A fitness center could run a Facebook ad campaign targeting local residents who have shown an interest in health and wellness. With clear call-to-actions and trackable results, social media advertising can be a powerful tool in your marketing arsenal.

Monitoring and Analytics

After a networking event, you'd likely reflect on the connections you made, the responses you received, and the overall impact on your business. Similarly, monitoring and analytics are crucial components of social media management.

Monitoring involves tracking your social media activities, such as likes, shares, comments, and followers. It can provide valuable feedback on what's resonating with your audience and where adjustments may be needed.

Analytics go a step further by providing in-depth insights into your audience demographics, best-performing content, website referrals, and more. It's like getting a detailed report card on your social media performance, offering valuable insights for future strategy.

In our ever-evolving digital age, social media is no longer optional; it's a must-have tool for businesses of all sizes. With the right choice of platforms, thoughtful content planning, strategic advertising, and diligent monitoring, you can leverage social media to connect with your audience, build your brand, and drive your business growth.

Over the past decade, the landscape of marketing on social media has undergone a significant transformation. Today, authenticity reigns supreme as the most engaging approach to presenting both yourself and your business online. Embracing this trend involves more than just being genuine; it's about strategically leveraging what sets you apart - your unique differentiators - and effectively showcasing these qualities across various platforms.

This new era of marketing emphasizes the importance of creating content that resonates with your audience on a personal level. It's about telling your story in a way that's not only true to your brand but also connects with the values and interests of your followers. Whether it's through behind-the-scenes glimpses, customer testimonials, or sharing your business journey, the key is to craft a narrative that's both relatable and distinctive.

Additionally, it's vital to understand the nuances of each social media platform and tailor your approach accordingly. What works on LinkedIn might not resonate on Instagram, and vice versa. This means adapting your message to fit the tone, style, and audience of each platform while maintaining a consistent brand voice.

Incorporating user-generated content, engaging directly with followers through comments and messages, and staying abreast of the latest trends and algorithm changes are also crucial components of an effective social media strategy. By doing so, you ensure that your brand not only stands out but also builds a loyal and engaged online community.

From understanding your customers and building a strong brand to developing effective marketing strategies and harnessing the power of social media, we've covered a lot of ground in this chapter. As we navigate the ever-evolving landscape of small business ownership, remember that marketing is not a standalone task; it's an integral part of your business strategy. It's about engaging your customers, showcasing your brand, and communicating your value in a way that resonates with your audience. Ponder on these insights, apply them in your business, and watch as your customer relationships flourish and your business thrives. As we move forward, we'll delve into the role of sales in driving business growth. Buckle up, as the road ahead is filled with potential and promise.

MARKET YOUR BUSINESS

- ☐ DO A CUSTOMER SEGMENTATION
- ☐ BUILD CUSTOMER FEEDBACK
- ☐ CREATE BRAND GUIDELINES
- ☐ LEARN MARKETING STRATEGIES
- ☐ BUILD SOCIAL MEDIA PROFILES
- ☐ REVIEW NETWORKING GROUPS

CHAPTER 6:

SELLING YOUR WAY TO SUCCESS: MASTERING THE SCIENCE AND SKILL OF SALES

"The most difficult thing is the decision to act. The rest is merely tenacity."
– Amelia Earhart

Have you ever watched a world-class athlete in action? There's a certain finesse, a blend of technique, strategy, and instinct that makes their performance captivating. Selling, at its best, is no different. It's a blend of understanding your buyer, managing your sales process, crafting an irresistible value proposition, and mastering the art of closing the deal.

6.1 THE SCIENCE OF SELLING

Understanding Buyer Psychology
Unlocking the door to successful sales begins with understanding the buyer's mind. It entails comprehending why people buy a desired product, how they make their decisions, and factors

that influence their choices. It's like being a detective, gathering clues, and piecing together the puzzle of your buyer's behavior.

Think about the last time you made a significant purchase. Perhaps you were buying a new laptop. Your decision was likely influenced by a combination of needs (e.g., performance, durability), emotional factors (e.g., brand reputation, aesthetics), and contextual elements (e.g., price, promotions). Unraveling these layers of buyer psychology can help you tailor your sales approach, connect with your customers on a deeper level, and effectively address their needs and desires.

Sales Funnel Management

A sales funnel (or customer journey map) is a visual representation of the buyer's journey, from the first point of contact with your business to the ultimate purchase decision. It's shaped like a funnel because as potential buyers move through the process, some drop out and only a fraction reach the end.

Managing your sales funnel effectively is like navigating a road trip. You need to know where you're starting, where you're heading, and what stops you'll make along the way. In the context of sales, this involves attracting prospects, nurturing them through the funnel, and ultimately converting them into customers.

For example, at the top of the funnel, you might attract prospects through social media marketing or content marketing. As these prospects show interest and enter the funnel, you might offer them valuable resources like whitepapers or webinars to nurture their interest. As they move further down the funnel, showing serious buying intent, you might offer personalized consultations or product demos to seal the deal.

Value Proposition Development

Your value proposition is a clear statement that explains how your product solves your customers' problems, delivers specific benefits, and tells the customer why they should buy from you and not from the competition. It's like your business's unique selling promise to your customers.

Consider, for example, a company that sells eco-friendly cleaning products. Their value proposition might emphasize the effectiveness of their products, commitment to environmental sustainability, and competitive pricing. This value proposition speaks directly to their target customers - individuals who are conscious about the environment and are looking for affordable, effective solutions.

Closing Techniques

Closing the sale is the final, crucial step in your sales process. It's like scoring the winning goal in a soccer match. You've navigated past the defenders (objections), you're near the goalpost (the purchase decision), and you need to take the shot (close the sale).

Closing techniques can vary based on the sales situation and customer. A direct close might work best when the customer is showing strong buying signals. In contrast, a summary close, where you recap the product's benefits to reinforce the value, might be more effective for complex sales.

For instance, if you're selling a gym membership and the prospect has expressed enthusiasm about getting fit, a direct close, such as "Would you like to start with a monthly or annual membership?" might seal the deal.

Selling, much like any skill, can be developed and honed over time. It requires understanding your buyer, managing your sales process, developing a compelling value proposition, and perfecting your closing techniques. With these tools in your arsenal, you can navigate the sales process with confidence and finesse, driving business growth and contributing to your bottom line. As we move forward, we'll explore the importance of building a robust sales process, training your sales team, and tracking and improving sales performance. Each of these components play a crucial role in your overall sales success. So, keep these insights in mind as you embark on your sales journey, and remember - every no brings you one step closer to a yes.

6.2 BUILDING A SALES PROCESS

Lead Generation Strategies

Envision a bustling farmer's market. As a vendor, your task is to attract potential buyers to your stall. You might do this by arranging your produce attractively, offering free samples, or advertising daily specials. In the realm of sales, this initial attraction phase is known as lead generation.

Lead generation strategies are about identifying and reaching out to potential customers, or 'leads'. These strategies can be as diverse as your business and can span both offline and online channels.

For instance, a real estate agency might generate leads through referrals from satisfied clients, by hosting informative webinars about the property market, or through targeted online advertising. The key is to understand where your potential customers are and how you can reach them effectively.

Sales Pitch Development

Once you've attracted potential buyers to your stall, the next step is to convince them to make a purchase. This involves explaining the benefits of your produce, answering questions, and perhaps even negotiating prices, which is your sales pitch.

Developing a compelling sales pitch involves clearly articulating the value of your product or service, addressing potential objections, and communicating why your offering is the best choice for the customer.

Consider a software development company pitching their services to a potential client. Their pitch might focus on their experienced team, past successful projects, their unique approach to software development, and how their services can solve the client's specific problems.

Follow-up Techniques

Let's say a customer shows interest in your produce but doesn't make a purchase. You might offer to send them a reminder about your next market appearance or invite them to visit your farm for a tour. These are follow-up techniques, designed to keep the conversation going and the interest alive.

In sales, effective follow-up techniques can mean the difference between a lost lead and a successful sale. This could involve sending a thank you email after a meeting, providing additional information as requested, or checking in after a few days to address any further questions.

For example, a car dealership might follow up with a potential customer by sending a personalized video showcasing the features of the car they were interested in, offering a test drive, or providing a competitive financing offer.

Sales Process Evaluation and Improvement

Finally, consider how you can improve your sales at the next farmer's market. In sales process and evaluation, you might assess which produce sold well, which lead generation strategies were effective, or how your sales pitch could be improved. In your business, this involves regularly reviewing and analyzing your sales activities, identifying what's working and what's not, and making necessary adjustments. This could involve tracking key sales metrics, soliciting feedback from customers, or conducting sales team debriefs.

For instance, a retail store might evaluate their sales process by analyzing their sales data to identify popular products, conducting customer surveys to understand their shopping experience, or providing sales training to improve team performance.

Building an effective sales process is a dynamic and iterative process. It's about finding what works for your business, continuously learning and adapting, and striving for improvement. As with any process, patience and persistence are key. Keep refining your process, connecting with your customers, and striving for sales success. With determination and strategic action, you're well-equipped to turn potential leads into loyal customers.

6.3 TRAINING YOUR SALES TEAM

Sales Training Program Development

Let's begin with the development of a sales training program. Imagine a play where actors are given scripts to study. They rehearse their lines, understand their characters, and learn their cues. The script and the rehearsals guide them to deliver a stellar performance. Similarly, a sales training program acts as a script for your sales team.

A well-structured sales training program should cover essential sales skills, product knowledge, customer understanding, and company ethos. It should also be tailored to the needs and experience levels of your sales team members.

For example, for a fitness equipment business, the training program might include modules on understanding different fitness needs, detailed product specifications, effective demonstration techniques, and handling common customer objections.

Role-Playing Scenarios

Role-playing is an effective training tool, much like athletes practicing their moves during training sessions. It allows your sales team members to rehearse their sales techniques, experiment with different approaches, and learn from their experiences in a safe, supportive environment.

Role-playing scenarios should reflect real-life sales situations your team members might encounter. For instance, in a software company, scenarios could include pitching to a tech-savvy client, dealing with price objections, or selling to a hesitant customer. By practicing these scenarios, your sales team can hone their skills, boost their confidence, and prepare for real-life sales situations.

Ongoing Training and Support

Sales training isn't a one-off event but an ongoing process. It's akin to maintaining a healthy diet. One nutritious meal won't make you healthy; it's what you eat consistently that counts. Similarly, ongoing training ensures that your sales team's skills remain sharp, and they are up-to-date with the latest sales strategies, market trends, and product updates.

Ongoing training can take various forms, such as regular workshops, one-on-one coaching sessions, or online courses. It should also provide support, such as access to resources, feedback sessions, and a platform to share experiences and learnings.

For example, a real estate agency might have weekly training sessions to discuss market trends, share successful sales strategies, and role-play challenging scenarios. They might also have a shared online resource hub, regular feedback sessions with the sales manager, and a team forum for sharing experiences and tips.

Performance-Based Incentives

Performance-based incentives act as a powerful motivator for your sales team. They're like the medals athletes earn when they perform exceptionally well. They not only reward high performance but also motivate the entire team to strive for excellence.

Performance-based incentives can range from commission or bonuses to non-monetary rewards like recognition, additional time off, or career advancement opportunities. The key is to align incentives with both individual and team performance goals and ensure they're perceived as fair and achievable.

For instance, a car dealership might offer a bonus for each car sold, an additional reward for reaching monthly targets, and a 'Salesperson of the Month' recognition for the highest performer. These incentives can motivate the sales team to put their training into practice and perform at their best.

Training your sales team is an investment for the success of your business, as it equips your team with the knowledge, skills, and motivation they need to convert leads into customers effectively. From developing a robust training program and using role-playing scenarios to providing ongoing training and performance-based incentives, these strategies can help you build a competent, confident, and high-performing sales team. So, as you navigate the exciting world of sales, remember that your team is your biggest asset, and their success is your success.

6.4 TRACKING AND IMPROVING SALES PERFORMANCE

Key Performance Indicators (KPIs)

Imagine an athlete rigorously preparing for a major competition, where monitoring speed, endurance, and strength becomes crucial to optimize performance. This analogy perfectly mirrors the role of Key Performance Indicators (KPIs) in the realm of sales. KPIs act as vital metrics that measure the effectiveness of sales efforts, providing valuable insights for continuous improvement and fine-tuning strategies.

The power of KPIs in sales lies in their ability to offer a clear, quantifiable view of performance in relation to set goals. These indicators are pivotal for identifying trends, forecasting future sales, and pinpointing areas needing enhancement. They ensure that a sales team's efforts are not only measurable but also aligned with the broader business objectives.

Selecting the right KPIs is a task that requires careful consideration and should be tailored to fit the specific context and objectives of the business. For example, a software company might prioritize tracking new subscriptions, customer retention rates, and average revenue per user. Other common KPIs in the sales sector include conversion rates, average deal size, lead response time, and the length of the sales cycle.

To effectively track these KPIs, implementing a sales scorecard or dashboard is highly beneficial. Such tools provide a real-time snapshot of performance, enabling quick, informed decision-making. A well-structured dashboard can integrate data from various sources, offering a comprehensive overview of all sales activities and outcomes. Moreover, these dashboards can be customized to spotlight the most relevant KPIs, ensuring focus on the metrics that matter most to the team and the business.

Regular analysis of KPIs paves the way for a dynamic and responsive sales management approach. By establishing benchmarks and comparing actual performance against these standards, businesses can discern their strengths and areas ripe for improvement. This process fosters a culture of continuous development, propelling teams towards higher levels of performance.

Integrating KPIs into the broader sales strategy is crucial. They should guide not only immediate tactics but also inform training programs, shaping a skilled and adaptable sales force. Linking incentives and rewards to key KPI achievements can further motivate teams, ensuring that their efforts are in sync with the overarching business goals.

In essence, KPIs in sales function much like a compass in the hands of a seasoned navigator, offering direction, charting progress, and guiding through the ever-changing dynamics of the sales landscape. Through the strategic use of a scorecard or dashboard for tracking these KPIs, businesses can turn data into actionable intelligence, propelling sales success and driving overall growth.

Sales Analytics Tools

Imagine a pilot navigating a plane. They rely on a dashboard of instruments, providing real-time information about altitude, speed, fuel levels, and more. Similarly, sales analytics tools act as your sales' dashboard, providing real-time insights into your sales performance.

Sales analytics tools can help you track your KPIs, monitor sales trends, and analyze individual and team performance. They can provide insights into customer behavior, sales cycle dynamics, and market trends. For example, a CRM (Customer Relationship Management) tool can provide detailed information about customer interactions, deal progress, and sales team activities.

Regular performance reviews are essential in any sales team, functioning similarly to a student's report card, which are crucial for providing your team with feedback that not only highlights their strengths but also pinpoints areas for improvement. This process is integral to enhancing both the quality of your team's work and your company's overall performance.

In these sessions, it's important to engage in a two-way conversation. They are opportunities to celebrate achievements, address challenges, and set meaningful goals. For instance, a retail manager might conduct monthly meetings with sales associates to review their sales performance, customer interactions, and set personal development objectives.

These reviews play a key role in fostering a culture of continuous improvement and open communication. They encourage team members to reflect on their contributions and align their goals with the company's objectives. Additionally, they offer managers a chance to provide tailored guidance and coaching, addressing specific needs and leveraging individual strengths.

By regularly conducting performance reviews, you not only boost your team's capabilities but also contribute significantly to the success and growth of your company.

Sales Improvement Strategies

Lastly, consider a gardener tending to a garden. They prune the plants, removing dead leaves and branches to stimulate new growth. Similarly, sales improvement strategies involve identifying and addressing areas of weakness in your sales process to stimulate growth and performance.

Sales improvement strategies can range from refining your sales process and enhancing your sales training program to revising your sales targets and incentive structures. The key is to base these strategies on insights derived from your KPIs, sales analytics, and performance reviews. For instance, if performance reviews reveal that closing deals is a common challenge for your sales team, you might offer a specialized training session on closing techniques.

Monitoring and enhancing sales performance is a continuous process, which entails keeping a pulse on your sales efforts, making data-driven decisions, and fostering a culture of continuous learning and improvement. With these strategies in place, you're well-positioned to optimize your sales performance and drive your business forward.

Over the past several chapters, we've covered a lot of ground. We've delved into the fundamentals of sales, from understanding the buyer's journey and developing a sales process to training your sales team and monitoring sales performance.

As you move forward, remember that sales are not a standalone function but an integral part of your business strategy. As you apply these insights in your business, you'll be well on your way to turning potential leads into loyal customers, driving business growth, and boosting your bottom line. As we move forward to the next chapter, we'll explore the distinction between working in your business and working on your business, and how finding the right balance can propel your small business to new heights.

MASTERING SALES

- ☐ CREATE A SALES FUNNEL
- ☐ LEARN CLOSING SKILLS
- ☐ DEVELOP YOUR SALES PITCH
- ☐ CREATE A TRAINING PROCESS
- ☐ DEVELOP INCENTIVE PROGRAM
- ☐ DETERMINE KPI'S
- ☐ SELECT CRM TOOL AND IMPLEMENT

CHAPTER 7:
LEADING FROM THE FRONT - NAVIGATING THE ENTREPRENEUR'S PATH

"Don't tell people how to do things, tell them what to do and let them surprise you with their results."
– George Patton

Picture a ship making its journey across vast open waters, its course dictated not by the hands-on deck but by the unseen captain below. This is the image of a business ensnared by the pitfalls of micromanagement, where the captain, the business owner, loses sight of the horizon, caught up in steering every minor operation.

The transition from being an individual contributor to a leader can be a significant shift. Many business owners find themselves inadvertently falling into the trap of micromanagement, driven by the desire to control every aspect of their business. However, micromanagement can create more problems than it solves.

Let's delve into the perils of micromanagement and how it can impact your business.

7.1 THE PERILS OF MICROMANAGEMENT

Employee Dissatisfaction

Imagine being an experienced painter, hired for your creative talent, but your employer insists on dictating every brushstroke. Over time, this constant oversight can lead to dissatisfaction and frustration.

In a business context, when employees are constantly monitored and given little autonomy, it can lead to a decrease in job satisfaction. Employees might feel that their abilities are not trusted, leading to a reduction in morale and overall job satisfaction. A study by Trinity Solutions, published in the book "My Way or the Highway", showed that 85% of respondents were affected by micromanagement.

Stifled Creativity

Consider a group of musicians that are all skilled in their craft. If their conductor insists on controlling every note, ignoring their creative input, the music produced may be technically correct but lacks the creative flair that makes it truly memorable.

Similarly, in a business setting, micromanagement can stifle creativity. When employees are not given the freedom to think outside the box and come up with innovative solutions, it can limit the potential for innovation. This can be particularly detrimental in roles or industries where creativity and innovation are key drivers of success.

Inefficient Use of Time

Picture a skilled architect who, instead of focusing on designing the structure's blueprint, is caught up in choosing the brick type for construction. The architect's time and skills are not being utilized efficiently.

In the same vein, when business owners micromanage, they spend time overseeing minor tasks that could be better spent on strategic decision-making or business development activities. This not only leads to inefficiency but can also slow down the decision-making process and limit the business's growth potential.

Reduced Trust

Think of a team sport like basketball. The team's success hinges on trust in each player's capabilities, understanding of the game, and execution of plays. If the coach were to question every pass and strategy, this trust would erode.

In a business environment, micromanagement can lead to reduced trust within the team. If employees feel that their every move is being watched and questioned, it can create an atmosphere of doubt and suspicion. This lack of trust can harm team relationships, reduce collaboration, and negatively impact the company culture.

In summary, while it might seem beneficial to have a tight grip on all business operations, micromanagement can lead to numerous negative consequences, including employee dissatisfaction, stifled creativity, inefficient use of time, and reduced trust. Avoiding these pitfalls is crucial for business growth and success. As we navigate further into this chapter, we will explore the importance of developing robust systems and processes, effective time management strategies, and the power of delegation as tools to avoid the trap of micromanagement.

7.2 SYSTEMS AND PROCESSES: THE BACKBONE OF YOUR BUSINESS

Running a business can sometimes feel like navigating a bustling railway station. Trains are arriving and departing, passengers are rushing to catch their connections, and amidst all the hustle and bustle, there's a precise system that keeps everything running smoothly. Likewise, your business operations hinge on well-defined systems and processes, keeping the wheels of your enterprise turning efficiently.

Standard Operating Procedures

Consider a well-rehearsed orchestra. Each musician knows their part, as each note contributes to the harmony, which, in turn, results to a seamless performance. This level of synchronization is achieved through meticulously outlined Standard Operating Procedures (SOPs), the conductor's score in the world of business.

SOPs serve as the blueprint for your business operations. They outline the sequence of steps to perform specific tasks, ensuring consistency, efficiency, and quality in your operations. For instance, a restaurant might have an SOP for preparing a particular dish, detailing the ingredients, preparation steps, cooking time, and presentation style. This SOP ensures that the dish is prepared consistently, regardless of who is cooking.

Automation Tools

Imagine trying to maintain a large garden using just a pair of gardening shears. It would be time-consuming and exhausting. Now, imagine having a set of power tools at your disposal. The task becomes much easier and efficient. This is the power of automation in your business.

Automation tools allow you to streamline routine tasks, saving time and reducing the risk of errors. For example, an e-commerce business might use automation tools to manage inventory, process orders, send out customer notifications, and generate sales reports. These tools free up valuable time that can be invested in strategic decision-making or customer engagement.

Quality Control Measures

Think of a potter meticulously shaping a piece of clay on a potter's wheel, smoothing out any imperfections to create a flawless pot. This attention to quality is crucial in business too. Quality control measures are your business's tools for smoothing out imperfections, ensuring your products or services meet the desired standards.

Quality control can involve various measures depending on your business type and industry. A manufacturing company might have quality checks at various stages of the production process. A software company might have rigorous testing protocols to ensure the software is bug-free and user-friendly. These quality control measures help maintain high standards, enhance customer satisfaction, and uphold your business's reputation.

Feedback Mechanisms

Finally, imagine a pilot flying a plane. The control panel provides continuous feedback about the plane's altitude, speed, and direction, helping the pilot make necessary adjustments. Similarly, feedback mechanisms in your business provide valuable insights, guiding your operational decisions.

Feedback can come from various sources - it can be your customers, employees, or even your own observations. For example, a coffee shop might have a suggestion box for customers, regular team meetings to gather employee feedback, and a system for monitoring service speed during peak hours. This feedback can help identify areas of improvement, leading to better operational efficiency and customer satisfaction.

In short, systems and processes are the backbone of your business operations. They provide the structure, efficiency, and control needed to run your business smoothly. By establishing robust SOPs, leveraging automation tools, implementing quality control measures, and utilizing feedback mechanisms, you can streamline your operations, enhance quality, and drive your business towards success.

7.3 TIME MANAGEMENT STRATEGIES FOR BUSINESS OWNERS

Imagine a conductor leading an orchestra. Each beat of the baton, each shift in tempo, and each pause is meticulously planned and executed. The result is a harmonious symphony, a testament to the power of precision and timing. Similarly, as a business owner, effective time management can be the conductor's baton that orchestrates your success.

Prioritization Techniques

Picture a bustling kitchen during dinner service. The chef, amidst the flurry of activity, must prioritize tasks to ensure each dish is prepared and served at the right time. Drawing from the same concept, prioritization is a critical time management strategy in running a business.

A popular method is the Eisenhower Matrix, a simple tool that helps you categorize tasks into four quadrants based on their urgency and importance.

- Quadrant 1: Important and Urgent. These are tasks that require immediate attention. For instance, responding to a customer complaint or addressing a product defect.
- Quadrant 2: Important but Not Urgent. These tasks are crucial for long-term success but do not require immediate action. Examples include strategic planning or employee training.
- Quadrant 3: Not Important but Urgent. These tasks can often be delegated. They might include attending a routine meeting or replying to non-urgent emails.
- Quadrant 4: Not Important and Not Urgent. These tasks are often distractions and should be minimized or eliminated. These could be activities like scrolling through social media or attending unnecessary meetings.

By understanding where each task fits into this matrix, you can better prioritize your time and focus on what truly matters.

Task Batching

Think of a factory assembly line. Instead of constructing a single product from start to finish, tasks are batched together for efficiency. You can apply a similar principle to manage your time more effectively.

Task batching involves grouping similar tasks together and completing them in one go. For example, you might dedicate a specific time each day to check and respond to emails, rather than responding to them sporadically throughout the day. Similarly, you could batch all your financial tasks, like invoicing or budgeting, into a specific day of the week.

By reducing the mental fatigue of constantly switching between tasks, you can enhance your focus, efficiency, and productivity.

Time Blocking

Imagine a city planner meticulously crafting a city layout, where each element – from neighborhoods to parks – is strategically placed for maximum efficiency and functionality. In the realm of time management, time blocking serves as your personal city planning tool, with your calendar being the central hub around which everything revolves.

Time blocking is the practice of segmenting your day into distinct blocks, each earmarked for a specific task or activity. For example, you might allocate the first hour of your day exclusively for strategic planning. This could be followed by a set period for team meetings, and then another block dedicated to customer engagements.

The key to effective time blocking is leveraging your calendar as the foundational tool. By scheduling these blocks in your calendar, you create a visual and structured plan of your day. This approach ensures that each task receives your full focus during its allotted time. It's a method that not only minimizes distractions but also boosts productivity and guarantees a well-balanced distribution of your time across various crucial activities.

Incorporating time blocking into your daily routine can transform the way you manage your tasks, helping you to navigate your workday with precision and purpose. By viewing your calendar as the cornerstone of this technique, you can achieve a higher level of organization and efficiency in your professional life.

Elimination of Time Wasters

Consider a gardener meticulously weeding a garden. By eliminating the weeds, they ensure that the plants get all the necessary nutrients, space, and sunlight to grow. In a similar vein, eliminating time wasters from your day can help you focus your time and energy on tasks that contribute to your business growth.

Time wasters could be unnecessary meetings, unproductive tasks, or even distractions like frequent email notifications or social media. By identifying and eliminating these time wasters, you can reclaim valuable time in your day to focus on high-priority tasks.

In conclusion, effective time management is about more than just being busy; it's being productive, understanding what tasks require your attention, when to tackle these tasks, and how to eliminate distractions that waste your time. By mastering these time management strategies, you can take control of your time and lead your business with increased efficiency, productivity, and success.

7.4 THE POWER OF DELEGATION

Delegating tasks is akin to a relay race. Each team member takes the baton, runs their part of the race, and passes it on to the next. When done right, the baton moves smoothly from one runner to the next, leading the team to victory. Similarly, effective delegation in your business can streamline operations, boost team performance, and drive business success. Let's look at how you can harness the power of delegation.

Identifying Tasks to Delegate

Think of a gardener pruning a tree. They decide which branches to trim, allowing the tree to focus its resources on the branches that bear fruit. In the same way, identifying tasks to delegate involves determining which tasks can be handled by others, allowing you to focus on tasks that require your expertise.

Tasks ideal for delegation typically fall into three categories. First, routine tasks such as data entry or scheduling appointments. Second, tasks outside your area of expertise, like accounting or graphic design. And finally, tasks that are a poor use of your time, perhaps because they can be done more efficiently or cost-effectively by someone else. Recognizing these tasks is your first step towards effective delegation.

Selecting the Right People

Imagine you're a movie director casting for a film. You wouldn't cast someone without considering their acting skills, suitability for the role, and their ability to bring the character to life. Similarly, selecting the right people to delegate to involves considering their skills, capabilities, and capacity.

You might have team members who are particularly skilled at organizing, making them ideal for managing schedules. While others might excel at detail-oriented tasks, making them a good fit for data-related tasks. By aligning tasks with your team's skills and capacities, you not only ensure tasks are done well but also empower your team members to work in their areas of strength.

Clear Communication of Expectations

Consider a composer conveying a musical piece to an orchestra. Simply handing out the sheet music isn't enough. The composer must share their vision for the piece, the mood they want to create, and how each instrument contributes to the overall performance. Similarly, when delegating tasks, clear communication of expectations is key.

This involves explaining the task clearly, defining the desired outcome, setting a deadline, and explaining how the task fits into the bigger picture. For instance, if you're delegating a market research task, you would explain the purpose of the research, the specific information required, the deadline, and how the research will inform future business decisions.

Follow-up and Feedback

Finally, imagine a coach guiding a sports team. The coach doesn't just assign positions and leave the team to their own devices; they provide ongoing direction, feedback, and encouragement. The same principle applies to delegation.

Follow-ups could involve regular check-ins to monitor progress, provide assistance, or address any issues. Feedback, on the other hand, is about acknowledging a job well done or providing constructive pointers for improvement. Remember, delegation is not about abdicating responsibility but about fostering a collaborative approach to achieving business goals.

In the quest for business success, delegation is your ally. It allows you to focus on what you do best, empowers your team, and drives productivity. So, take the leap, delegate wisely, and watch as your team - and your business thrive.

As we navigate the thrilling realm of entrepreneurship, remember that your role as a business owner is not just about managing tasks; it's about leading your team towards a shared vision, building robust systems, managing your time effectively, and harnessing the power of delegation. With these strategies at your disposal, you're well-equipped to lead from the front, steering your business ship towards the shores of success. As we chart our course forward, we will explore the exciting prospect of scaling your business, a journey filled with opportunities, challenges, and immense potential.

LEADING FROM THE FRONT

- ☐ **LEARN ABOUT PERILS**
- ☐ **BUILD SOP'S**
- ☐ **IMPLEMENT AUTOMATION**
- ☐ **OPTIMIZE FEEDBACK LOOPS**
- ☐ **BUILD PRIORITY STACKS**
- ☐ **LEVERAGE YOUR CALENDAR**
- ☐ **COMMUNICATE EXPECTATIONS**

CHAPTER 8:

SCALING YOUR BUSINESS: TIMING, PREPARATION, AND EXECUTION

"Don't let the fear of striking out hold you back."
– Babe Ruth

Imagine standing on the edge of a diving board, high above the pool. You feel the solid platform under your feet, hear the echo of voices around the pool, and see the shimmering water below. You've practiced your dive countless times, honed your technique, and built your strength. Now, the only question is - are you ready to make the leap?

Scaling your business is much like standing on that diving board. It's an exciting prospect, filled with potential. But it's also a significant leap, requiring preparation, timing, and execution. And just like diving, the success of your scaling efforts often hinges on knowing when you're ready to take the plunge. Let's explore the signs that your business might be ready to scale.

8.1 WHEN TO SCALE: SIGNS YOU'RE READY

Consistent Revenue Growth

Think of a baker kneading dough. As they knead, the dough expands, growing in size. This consistent growth is a positive sign, indicating that the dough is developing the right structure for baking. In the same manner, consistent revenue growth in your business is a positive sign, indicating that your business model is working and that there is a steady demand for your product or service.

Consistent revenue growth shows that your business is generating a steady stream of income over time. It's not just about having one good month or quarter; it's about seeing a pattern of growth. This shows that your business has a solid customer base and is successfully converting leads into sales.

Stable Market Conditions

Imagine planning a picnic. You would likely check the weather forecast to ensure a sunny, calm day. Just as you wouldn't plan a picnic in the middle of a thunderstorm, you wouldn't want to scale your business in the midst of unstable market conditions.

Before scaling, ensure that the market conditions are favorable. This means there is steady demand for your product or service, the economy is stable, and there are no significant market fluctuations that could impact your business. It's also important to consider the competitive landscape and ensure there is room for your business to grow.

Strong Team in Place

Consider a construction project. Before the builders start adding the upper floors, they make sure the foundation is solid and the supporting structures are secure. Similarly, before scaling your business, it's crucial to have a strong team in place.

A strong team is one that is skilled, committed, and capable of managing increased workload. They understand your business values, are aligned with your business goals, and can work together efficiently. Before scaling, ensure that you have the right people in the right roles, and that they are ready and equipped to handle the growth.

Scalable Infrastructure

Picture a town preparing for a large festival. The town officials ensure that the infrastructure - roads, public transport, utilities - can handle the increased traffic and activity. Likewise, before scaling your business, you need to ensure that your business infrastructure can handle increased activity.

Scalable infrastructure could include physical aspects like office space or production facilities, as well as virtual aspects, like software systems or online platforms. Prior to scaling, review your infrastructure to identify any areas that might need to be upgraded or expanded to support business growth.

In conclusion, scaling your business is a significant step, not to be taken lightly. It requires careful consideration and preparation. Before making the leap, look for signs that your business is ready - consistent revenue growth, stable market conditions, a strong team, and scalable infrastructure. These signs indicate that your business has the potential to soar to greater heights, much like a well-prepared diver leaping off the board, ready to make a splash.

8.2 FINANCING YOUR GROWTH

Financing growth is akin to fueling a rocket preparing for launch; it's about securing the resources that will power your business to new heights. The type of fuel you choose depends on your business's unique requirements and circumstances. Let's explore some of your options.

Bootstrapping

Bootstrapping is the business equivalent of a self-funded road trip. It involves funding your business's growth using your own resources or the business's profits. This strategy allows you to maintain full control over your business as you're not beholden to investors or lenders.

For example, if you run a successful bakery, you might decide to use the profits from your existing operations to open a second location. This would be a form of bootstrapping.

However, bootstrapping might limit your growth speed as you're limited by the number of profits you can reinvest. It's also worth noting that bootstrapping can put personal finances at risk if the business encounters financial difficulties.

Business Loans

Securing a business loan is like taking a taxi to your destination. The taxi (or in this case, the lender) provides the necessary fuel (funds), but you'll need to pay it back with interest.

Business loans can be obtained from various sources, including banks, credit unions, and online lenders. They can provide a significant financial boost, allowing you to undertake larger growth projects such as buying new equipment, expanding your premises, or increasing your product range.

However, business loans require good credit history and often require collateral. Additionally, interest and repayment terms can add to your business's financial burden, so it's essential to assess the loan's terms carefully.

Venture Capital

Venture capital funding is akin to inviting passengers on your trip, who are willing to contribute to the fuel costs in exchange for a share of the experience. In business terms, venture capitalists invest in your business in exchange for equity, providing the funds you need to scale.

Venture capitalists often bring more than just money to the table. They can also provide industry expertise, strategic guidance, and valuable networks. For example, a tech startup might secure venture capital funding to develop a new app, benefiting from the venture capitalist's industry knowledge and connections.

However, in exchange for their investment, venture capitalists often require a stake in your business, which means you'll need to share control and profits. They also typically seek high-growth businesses with a viable exit strategy, so this option might not be suitable for all types of businesses.

Crowdfunding

Crowdfunding is like inviting a group of friends to chip in for a shared adventure. Each friend contributes a small amount, and together, they fund the trip. In the business world, crowdfunding involves raising small amounts of money from a large number of people, typically via online platforms.

Crowdfunding can be a viable way to finance your growth, especially if your business has a strong brand and a compelling story that resonates with the public. For instance, an eco-friendly clothing brand might launch a crowdfunding campaign to finance a new line of sustainable apparel.

There are different types of crowdfunding, including donation-based, rewards-based, and equity crowdfunding. Each comes with its own set of rules and considerations, so it's important to choose the right type for your business.

In conclusion, financing your growth is a critical aspect of scaling your business. Whether you choose to bootstrap, secure a business loan, seek venture capital, or go the crowdfunding route, each option comes with its own set of benefits and considerations. By understanding these options and assessing them against your business's needs and goals, you can choose the right 'fuel' to power your business's growth.

8.3 BUILDING SCALABLE SYSTEMS

Scaling a business isn't just about increasing your workforce or expanding your product line. It also involves building systems that can accommodate and support that growth. When these systems are scalable, they can effortlessly handle increasing demands, ensuring the smooth operation of your business even as it grows. Let's explore four key aspects of building scalable systems: adopting cloud-based solutions, developing scalable marketing strategies, outsourcing non-core functions, and implementing advanced analytics.

Cloud-Based Solutions

Imagine your business data as a vast library of books. As the library grows, you need more space to store the books and a more efficient system to organize and retrieve them. In the digital world, cloud-based solutions provide that space and efficiency, offering a flexible and scalable solution for data storage and management.

Cloud-based solutions, such as cloud storage, cloud computing, and Software as a Service (SaaS), offer the ability to scale up or down as your business needs change. For instance, as your customer data grows, cloud storage can easily be expanded to accommodate it. Similarly, as your team grows, additional users can be added to your cloud-based software applications.

Embracing cloud-based solutions not only supports scalability but also enhances collaboration, as team members can access data and applications from anywhere. It also reduces the need for extensive on-premise IT infrastructure, saving costs and simplifying IT management.

Scalable Marketing Strategies

Consider your marketing efforts as a series of roads leading customers to your business. As your business grows, you'll need to build wider roads, or even highways, to bring in more traffic. Scalable marketing strategies are those highways, designed to attract and engage an increasing number of customers as your business grows.

A scalable marketing strategy might involve leveraging digital marketing channels like social media, email marketing, and search engine marketing. These channels can reach a large audience and can easily be scaled up by increasing your ad spend or expanding your campaigns.

Another scalable marketing strategy is content marketing. By creating valuable content, you can attract and engage a growing audience, driving traffic to your website and generating leads. As your content library grows, it continues to attract visitors, providing a long-term return on investment.

Outsourcing Non-Core Functions

Imagine running a theater production. You could try to write the script, design the costumes, and play all the roles yourself. But the play would likely be more successful if you focused on your strengths, say, directing the play and outsourcing the other tasks to skilled professionals.

In the same way, outsourcing non-core functions allows you to focus on what you do best while benefiting from the expertise of specialists. Non-core functions could include tasks like accounting, human resources, or IT support.

Outsourcing not only frees up your time but also provides access to expert knowledge, and can be scaled up or down as needed. For example, you might start by outsourcing your accounting to a freelance professional, then scale up to a full-service accounting firm as your business grows.

Implementing Advanced Analytics

Think of advanced analytics as a high-powered telescope allowing you to see far into the distance and spot approaching opportunities and obstacles. In a business context, advanced analytics tools can provide in-depth insights into your business performance, customer behavior, and market trends, guiding your decision-making as your business grows.

Advanced analytics involves using sophisticated tools and techniques to analyze large volumes of data, uncover patterns and correlations, and predict future trends. As your business scales and you collect more data, these insights become increasingly valuable.

For instance, you might use advanced analytics to identify which customer segments are driving your growth, which marketing strategies are most effective, or how changes in the market could impact your business. These insights can inform your strategic planning, helping you navigate the path of scaling your business.

Building scalable systems is like laying down tracks for a train, guiding your business growth in the right direction. While the journey of scaling your business can be challenging, with the right systems in place, you'll be well-equipped to handle the increased speed and load, steering your business towards new horizons of success and prosperity.

8.4 NAVIGATING THE CHALLENGES OF SCALING

Scaling your business is akin to sailing into uncharted waters. It's thrilling and full of opportunity, but it also comes with its share of challenges. Let's set sail and explore how to navigate these challenges successfully.

Maintaining Company Culture

Picture your business culture as a vibrant tapestry. Each thread represents a value, tradition, shared understanding that binds your team together. As your business grows, it's crucial to maintain this tapestry, ensuring that your company culture remains intact.

Maintaining company culture amid growth involves reinforcing your core values, fostering open communication, and preserving a sense of camaraderie within your expanding team. For example, you might hold regular team-building events, create channels for transparent communication, and take the time to celebrate milestones and successes together. It's about creating an environment where each new member feels welcomed and each existing member feels valued.

Managing Increased Workload

Think of scaling your business as tuning a musical instrument. As you tighten the strings to reach a higher pitch, you also increase the tension. In the same way, scaling your business often involves managing an increased workload, which brings its own set of stresses and strains.

Managing this increased workload effectively requires careful planning, efficient systems, and a resilient team. You might need to streamline your operations, automate routine tasks, or hire additional team members. Remember, it's not just about working harder, but also working smarter.

Ensuring Quality Control

Consider a chef in a busy restaurant. As the orders pile up, the chef must ensure that each dish maintains the same high standard of quality, regardless of the volume. Similarly, as your business scales, ensuring quality control becomes even more critical.

Quality control during scaling might involve implementing standardized processes, conducting regular quality checks, and providing ongoing training for your team. It's about ensuring that your product or service remains consistent in quality, no matter how much your business grows.

Retaining Customer Satisfaction

Imagine a bustling café where each customer feels welcomed, served promptly, and leaves satisfied. As the café becomes more popular, the challenge is to maintain this level of customer satisfaction, despite the increased customer volume. The same principle applies when scaling your business.

Retaining customer satisfaction as your business grows requires a customer-centric approach, efficient customer service systems, and a team committed to customer satisfaction. You might need to enhance your customer service team, implement a customer relationship management system, or provide additional training to your team. After all, happy customers are the lifeblood of any business, big or small.

Scaling your business is not a destination but a voyage. It's a voyage that calls for courage, preparation, and the ability to navigate through challenges. As you steer your business towards growth, remember to maintain your company culture, manage the increased workload, ensure quality control, and retain customer satisfaction. These are your guiding stars, helping you navigate the exciting voyage of scaling your business. As we continue exploring the world of entrepreneurship, we'll delve into the realm of innovation and adaptation, crucial elements for the long-term success of any business.

CHAPTER 9:

KEEPING AHEAD OF THE CURVE: FOSTERING INNOVATION AND ADAPTABILITY

"The secret of change is to focus all of your energy, not on fighting the old, but building on the new."
– Socrates

Imagine standing atop a hill, overlooking a vast landscape. You see places that are familiar - the town where your business is, the roads you've traveled. But you also see the unfamiliar - new terrains, unexplored territories. As a small business owner, you're constantly navigating between the known and the unknown, balancing the comfort of what's tried-and-tested with the thrill of what's new and innovative. And in today's fast-paced, ever-changing business landscape, this balance isn't just a luxury; it's a necessity.

Innovation and adaptability are the dual engines that power long-term business success. In this chapter, we'll explore how you can fuel these engines in your small business, from understanding the importance of innovation and fostering a culture of creativity, to adapting to market changes and embracing technological advances. Let's begin by understanding why innovation is crucial for your small business.

9.1 THE IMPORTANCE OF INNOVATION IN SMALL BUSINESS

Competitive Advantage

Think of a bustling marketplace, where multiple vendors vie for the attention of customers. Now, imagine a vendor offering something unique, something no other vendor has. This vendor would naturally stand out, drawing more customers towards them. This is the power of innovation in giving your business a competitive edge.

Innovation can differentiate your business from competitors, making you stand out in the crowded marketplace. Whether it's a novel product, a unique service approach, or a groundbreaking business model, innovation sets you apart. It's like having a distinctive signboard in a crowded market - it catches attention, piques interest, and draws customers towards your business.

Increased Market Share

Consider a game of chess. The player who controls the center of the board often has an advantage, able to move their pieces more freely and dictate the game's pace. Similarly, innovation can help your business control more 'squares' on the business 'chessboard,' increasing your market share.

Innovative businesses often attract more customers, capturing a larger slice of the market pie. They offer something new and valuable to customers, something they can't get elsewhere. As a result, customers are drawn to these businesses, helping them increase their market share.

Enhanced Customer Experience

Imagine walking into a store and being greeted by a friendly shopkeeper who knows your name, remembers your usual order, and makes recommendations based on your preferences. This personalized, memorable experience would likely make you a loyal customer. This is the impact innovation can have on the customer experience.

Innovation isn't just about creating new products or services; it's also about enhancing the way customers interact with your business. This could involve creating a user-friendly website, offering personalized customer service, or implementing a seamless online checkout process. These innovations enhance the customer experience, building customer satisfaction and loyalty.

Long-Term Business Survival

Picture a tree adapting to the seasons, shedding its leaves in autumn to conserve resources for the winter, and blossoming in spring when conditions are favorable. Just like this tree, businesses need to adapt and innovate to survive in the long term.

In today's fast-paced business environment, change is the only constant. Customer preferences evolve, new competitors enter the market, and technological advances redefine industries. In the face of these changes, businesses that innovate and adapt are the ones that thrive. They stay relevant, meet emerging customer needs, and turn challenges into opportunities.

In conclusion, innovation plays a pivotal role in enhancing your competitive advantage, increasing your market share, enhancing the customer experience, and ensuring your business's long-term survival. It's like a compass, guiding your business through the ever-changing landscape of the small business ecosystem. As we navigate further into this chapter, we'll explore how to foster a culture of innovation in your business, turning it into a hotbed of creative ideas and innovative solutions.

9.2 FOSTERING A CULTURE OF INNOVATION

Encouraging Idea Sharing

Imagine a brainstorming session where every team member feels valued and heard. Their ideas, no matter how outlandish, are welcomed with enthusiasm. This environment of openness and acceptance is conducive to innovation. It is an atmosphere where possibilities are endless and creativity is encouraged.

In your small business, foster a similar setting. Create a platform for your team members to voice their thoughts and suggestions. This could be through regular brainstorming sessions, an online idea board, or simply an open-door policy. Make sure your team knows that every idea is valuable and that their contribution matters.

For instance, a small design agency might hold weekly brainstorming sessions where team members can share their ideas for new design techniques or process improvements. This not only fuels innovation but also builds a sense of ownership and engagement among team members.

Rewarding Creative Thinking

Consider a child who receives praise for a well-done painting. The positive reinforcement not only brings joy but also encourages the child to continue creating. In the same way, rewarding creative thinking in your business can stimulate continuous innovation.

Develop a recognition system that celebrates creative ideas and innovative solutions. This doesn't necessarily have to be a monetary reward. It could be as simple as mentioning the person's contribution in a team meeting or featuring them in a company newsletter. The goal is to show appreciation and reinforce the value of creative thinking.

For example, a tech startup could have an "Innovator of the Month" program, recognizing an employee who has proposed an innovative solution or idea. This not only incentivizes innovation but also fosters a culture of creativity within the company.

Providing Time for Innovation

Think back to your school days, when a period was often dedicated to creative pursuits like painting or crafting. This specific time allocated for creativity allowed for exploration and innovation. In the same vein, providing time for innovation in your business can lead to surprising results.

Allocate specific 'innovation time' where your team members can step away from their regular tasks and focus on creative problem-solving or idea generation. This gives them the freedom to think, explore, and innovate without the pressure of daily tasks.

For instance, a marketing firm might allow team members to dedicate a few hours each week to work on innovative projects or learn new skills. This 'innovation time' can lead to new service offerings, process improvements, or even new business ventures.

Implementing Innovative Ideas

Visualize a potter's wheel. The potter shapes and molds the clay, but the process doesn't stop there. The clay must be fired in a kiln to transform it into a sturdy, usable object. Similarly, coming up with innovative ideas is just the first step. The next crucial step is implementing these ideas, transforming them from abstract concepts into tangible improvements.

Create a process for evaluating, testing, and implementing the ideas generated by your team. This could involve a team discussion to evaluate the feasibility of the idea, a small-scale test to assess its effectiveness, and a plan for company-wide implementation if the test is successful.

For example, a software company might implement an innovative idea for a new feature in their product. After discussing the idea and assessing its feasibility, they could develop a prototype, test it with a few key clients, and if the feedback is positive, roll it out to all users.

In conclusion, fostering a culture of innovation is about creating an environment that encourages idea sharing, rewards creative thinking, provides time for innovation, and implements innovative ideas. This culture serves as fertile ground, planting the seeds of innovation that can grow and flourish, propelling your business towards long-term success.

9.3 ADAPTING TO MARKET CHANGES

Regular Market Research

Picture yourself as a seasoned surfer, attuned to the rhythm of the waves. Just as a surfer studies the ocean's patterns to catch the perfect wave, regular market research allows you to understand and navigate the ebbs and flows of your business landscape.

Market research involves gathering and analyzing information about your industry, competition, and customers. It's like putting on a pair of binoculars, enabling you to spot trends, identify opportunities, and foresee challenges.

Consider the owner of a health food store. Regular market research might involve tracking health and wellness trends, monitoring competitors' offerings, and surveying customers about their dietary preferences. This ongoing research keeps the business owner informed, enabling them to adapt their product range, marketing strategies, and store operations as the market changes.

Swift Implementation of Changes

Think of a skilled soccer player swiftly changing direction to outwit their opponent. In the same way, the ability to implement changes swiftly can give your business a competitive edge.

When market research reveals a need for change, acting quickly can make all the difference. It's about being nimble and responsive, adjusting your strategies and operations to align with market changes.

Take the example of a software development company. If regular market research reveals a growing demand for a particular feature, swift implementation could involve developing a prototype, testing it with a select group of users, and rolling it out to all users. The ability to adapt swiftly to market changes can enhance customer satisfaction, make you ahead of competitors, and drive business growth.

Customer Feedback Analysis

Imagine running a theater and receiving reviews after each performance. Analyzing these reviews can provide valuable insights, helping you fine-tune the script, improve the performance, and deliver a better experience for the audience. Similarly, in the business world, customer feedback analysis is a crucial tool for adapting to market changes.

Customer feedback can reveal what's working, what's not, and what could be improved. It's a direct line to your customers' needs, preferences, and experiences, providing invaluable insights for your business.

For instance, a restaurant owner might analyze customer feedback from online reviews, comment cards, and social media. This feedback can reveal popular dishes, areas for service improvement, or even new menu ideas, guiding the restaurant's adaptation to changing customer tastes and expectations.

Continuous Learning and Development

Consider a professional athlete, continuously training, learning, and improving to stay at the top of their game. Similarly, in the dynamic world of small business, continuous learning and development are key to staying abreast of market changes.

Continuous learning involves staying up-to-date with industry news, attending relevant seminars or workshops, and learning from thought leaders in your field. Development, on the other hand, involves applying this learning to improve your business operations, strategies, and offerings.

For example, a small business consultant might engage in continuous learning by attending industry conferences, participating in online courses, and following influential business blogs. They might apply this learning to develop their consulting methodologies, enhance their service offerings, and provide more value to their clients.

In conclusion, adapting to market changes is about staying alert, being responsive, listening to your customers, and committing to continuous improvement. It's a dynamic and ongoing process, but with the right strategies, you can navigate market changes with agility and confidence, keeping your business on the path to long-term success.

9.4 EMBRACING TECHNOLOGICAL ADVANCES

Look around you. The digital age is upon us, and technology is woven into the very fabric of our lives. From the way we communicate to how we shop, learn, and work, technology has revolutionized our world. For small businesses, this digital revolution presents a wealth of opportunities. It's like opening a box filled with advanced tools, each designed to optimize a different aspect of your business. In this section, we'll explore four key areas where technology can power your small business growth - social media platforms, e-commerce solutions, data analytics, and remote work technologies.

Utilizing Social Media Platforms

Think of social media platforms as bustling town squares. They're places where people gather to exchange news, share experiences, and connect with others. For businesses, these platforms offer unique opportunities to engage with customers, build brand awareness, and drive business growth.

The key to utilizing social media platforms effectively is to understand where your customers spend their time and how you can engage them on those platforms. This might involve sharing valuable content, engaging in conversations, and responding to customer inquiries or feedback.

For instance, a fitness studio might use Instagram to share workout tips, client success stories, and class schedules. They might engage with their followers by responding to comments, participating in relevant hashtags, and collaborating with fitness influencers. By utilizing social media platforms effectively, the studio can build a vibrant online community, attract new clients, and strengthen relationships with existing clients.

Implementing E-commerce Solutions

Imagine a traditional brick-and-mortar store deciding to set up an online shop. This expansion into the digital realm can open up new markets, increase sales, and enhance customer convenience. Similarly, implementing e-commerce solutions can provide a significant boost for your small business.

E-commerce solutions can range from setting up an online store and implementing secure payment systems to optimizing your website for mobile shopping and offering customer support via live chat. These solutions can help you reach customers beyond your geographical location, provide a convenient shopping experience, and operate your business 24/7.

For example, a local artisan might implement an e-commerce solution to sell their handcrafted products online. This could involve setting up an online shop on a platform like Etsy, offering secure payment options, and providing customer support via email and social media. By embracing e-commerce, the artisan can reach a global customer base, increase their sales, and grow their business.

Leveraging Data Analytics

Consider a ship captain navigating the seas. They rely on their compass, map, and weather data to chart the best course. In the world of small business, data analytics are your navigational tools, guiding your business decisions and strategies.

Data analytics involves collecting, analyzing, and interpreting data to gain insights about your business performance, customer behavior, and market trends. These insights can inform your business decisions, helping you identify opportunities, address challenges, and optimize your business operations.

For instance, an online retailer might leverage data analytics to understand their customers' purchasing behavior, identify popular products, and forecast sales trends. These insights can guide the retailer's inventory management, marketing strategies, and product development, driving informed decision-making and business growth.

Adopting Remote Work Technologies

Imagine a traditional office transforming into a virtual workspace, where team members can collaborate from different locations and time zones. This transformation, made possible by remote work technologies, can offer numerous benefits for your small business.

Remote work technologies can range from communication tools like email and video conferencing to collaboration tools like project management software and cloud-based applications. These technologies can enable your team to work flexibly and efficiently, reduce overhead costs, and access a wider talent pool.

For example, a digital marketing agency might adopt remote work technologies to operate a virtual team. They might use email and video conferencing for communication, a project management tool for coordinating tasks, and cloud-based software for creating and sharing work. By adopting remote work technologies, the agency can operate efficiently and flexibly, catering to clients worldwide.

In conclusion, embracing technological advances is like equipping your business with a set of powerful tools. These tools can help you engage with customers, expand your market, make informed decisions, and operate efficiently. As you navigate the path of small business ownership, remember that technology is your ally, propelling you towards greater success and prosperity. As we continue our exploration of the small business landscape, we'll delve into the exciting realm of innovation and adaptation, crucial for staying ahead of the curve in today's dynamic business environment.

CONCLUSION

Finally, we've arrived at the end of our shared journey through the roadmap to small business success. But as the saying goes, every end is just a new beginning. Together, we've embarked on a voyage of discovery, exploring the many facets of running a successful small business - from crafting a compelling vision and building a robust business plan, to navigating the challenges of scaling and fostering a culture of innovation.

As an entrepreneur myself, I've walked in your shoes and felt the same exhilaration and anxiety that comes with owning a business. It's a journey filled with both challenges and triumphs. But remember, every challenge is an opportunity for growth, and every triumph is a testament to your resilience and determination.

The key takeaways we've discussed throughout this book, your playbook for business mastery, are not just theoretical concepts, but practical tools tested in the crucible of real-life business scenarios. They are the lessons I've learned from my own experience and the wisdom I've gleaned from successful business leaders over the years.

From understanding your customers and building a strong brand, to mastering the art of delegation and adapting to market changes, each chapter has equipped you with the knowledge and insights needed to navigate the complex and exciting world of small business ownership.

But remember, knowledge is only powerful when applied. So, I encourage you to take these insights, apply them in your business, and witness the transformation they can bring. Use this book as a reference, guide, and friend who's there to support you every step of the way.

Now, it's your turn to take the reins. Your journey to business mastery awaits. I invite you to roll up your sleeves, step into your leadership role, and guide your business to new heights. Apply the strategies, use the tools, and trust in your ability to lead.

Remember, you are not alone on this journey. I've been there, and I believe in your potential to create a successful and fulfilling business. So go ahead, take that leap, and embark on your journey to business mastery. I can't wait to see where this road takes you.

And as you set sail, remember these words: "Success is not the destination, it's the journey." So, enjoy the ride, learn from each experience, and celebrate every milestone. You've got this!

Dear Reader!

Thank you sincerely for investing your time in reading 'The Small Business Playbook.' I hope the insights and stories within these pages have inspired you and provided valuable perspectives on leadership, visioning, and business strategy.

If you're motivated to explore tailored leadership coaching further, especially designed for small businesses and executives, I'm here to guide you. My coaching is customized for companies with $1M to $25M in revenue and includes expertise in EOS® self-implementation, ensuring your leadership journey is as impactful as possible.

Connect With Me for Custom Leadership Coaching
Take the next step in transforming your leadership style and business success. Scan the QR code below to connect with me directly. This will lead you to a contact form on my website, where we can start a conversation about your specific coaching needs and how we can achieve your business goals together.

Scan this code to begin your journey in custom leadership coaching and unlock the full potential of your business.

I'm looking forward to the opportunity to work with you and witness your growth and success.

Scan me!

Sincerely,

Pete Srodoski
Author and Head Business Coach